"*Winning Golf* provides readers with several practical training exercises that they can put into use immediately to improve their scores. The compilation of mental advice by Dr. Miller, with input from world class athletes and yesterday's and today's stars, makes the book entertaining and relevant. It is a must read for any level of golfer trying to bring their game to the next level!"— **Derek Sprague**, past president of the PGA of America and general manager of TPC Sawgrass, Ponte Vedra Beach, FL

"Saul Miller brings to bear his extensive experience working with athletes from many sports on ways of rising to the mental challenges that golf provides. He has worked with golfers of all abilities, studied how the best players manage themselves and their games, and offers practical suggestions for a winning mental game. If you want to develop what Dr. Miller terms 'right feeling, right focus, and right attitude,' this is the book for you." — **Lorne Rubenstein**, author with Tiger Woods of *The 1997 Masters: My Story* and winner of the PGA of America's Lifetime Achievement Award in Journalism

"Golf is a game where you can go from feeling very relaxed to experiencing stress within minutes. Conscious breathing is just one technique Dr. Miller describes in this fascinating book that will help everyone reduce their stress level before an important shot and generally play with more consistency and impact."— **Bob Gelesko**, Golf Professional, Rams Hill Country Club, Borrego Springs, CA

"Guaranteed to improve you as a player! *Winning Golf* simplifies the mental game and has many practical applications for everyday life." — **Eric Wang**, CPGA Teaching Professional, Victoria Golf Academy

"*Winning Golf: The Mental Game* provides great insight into the mental side of succeeding on the golf course and in everyday life. Saul has really touched on several areas where high level players and weekend warriors struggle whether they actually realize it or not. A great read and for me a great tune up to regain my mental edge on the course." — **Rhein Gibson**, PGA Tour Pro and Guinness record holder of the lowest score in a round (55)

"Dr. Saul Miller has written another wonderful book about the intricacies of performing at the highest levels. He has worked with many athletes from many different sports and has helped them to realize the importance of understanding themselves, their emotions, their minds and, most importantly, the intimate connection of mind and body.

Winning Golf dives into the golfer's mindset: an area that is so often overlooked. It offers some real solutions to performance anxiety. There's also great advice from golfers, as well as athletes in other sports, regarding improving performance by developing greater self-awareness. Being a player who competed at the highest levels, I always knew how important the mind is, and I read numerous books on the subject. Every golfer who wants to succeed to the best of their abilities must include the knowledge of how the mind/body connection works. Dr. Saul does a good job of bringing the player back to 'center' with mindful breathing. Yes, it takes discipline — anything worthwhile does. This is a book that every serious golfer needs to have on his or her bookshelf to help start on this journey of self-awareness that is so important not only in golf, but in life." — **Jim Nelford**, Lifetime Member of the PGA Tour, TV golf analyst, innovative instructor, and member of Canada's Golf Hall of Fame

"Dr. Saul's techniques helped me play the best hockey of my career, particularly during our winning Stanley Cup season. These techniques continue to serve me in life and on the golf course. Reading *Winning Golf* and continuing to work on the exercises prescribed will improve your performance and pleasure playing golf." — **Bret Hedican**, 17-year NHL veteran, two-time Olympian, TV broadcaster, and recreational golfer

"I enjoyed working with Dr. Saul Miller in my formative years as a professional on the PGA Tour. Saul's book, *Winning Golf: The Mental Game*, is an excellent resource for a better understanding of the mental side of golf performance. I highly recommend reading and following Saul's guidance." — **Richard Zokol**, PGA Tour winner, member of Canada's Golf Hall of Fame, and MindTRAK creator

"Dr. Miller's book *Winning Golf* is a must-read for all golfers and covers all the internal challenges we confront in the game of golf on a daily basis." — **Keith Maxwell**, PGA Professional, Sunningdale Golf Club, Berkshire, England

"This is a very clear, comprehensive, and well-organized approach to developing a player's mental game. Any serious competitor would do well to follow Miller's suggestions and practice his exercises as much as they work on their mechanics and their physical fitness. I will recommend this work to everyone and I think it could be especially useful to young kids who are mature enough. It's a great plan for life in general." — **Jim Petralia**, member of the California PGA Teaching Hall of Fame and one of *Golf Magazine*'s top 50 American instructors

"*Winning Golf: The Mental Game* will improve the quality of your golf . . . and your life. Trust me, this stuff really works." — **Cliff Ronning**, 18-year NHL veteran and sub-70 recreational golfer

"This book can help you to strengthen your mental game and play happier, better golf." — **Nancy Lopez**, a true golf icon, LPGA and World Golf Hall of Fame member (48 LPGA victories)

WINNING GOLF

THE MENTAL GAME

(CREATING THE FOCUS, FEELING,
AND CONFIDENCE TO PLAY
CONSISTENTLY WELL)

DR. SAUL L. MILLER

SPORT AND PERFORMANCE PSYCHOLOGIST

This book is also available as a Global Certified Accessible™ (GCA) ebook. ECW Press's ebooks are screen reader friendly and are built to meet the needs of those who are unable to read standard print due to blindness, low vision, dyslexia, or a physical disability.

Purchase the print edition and receive the eBook free. For details, go to ecwpress.com/eBook.

Published by ECW Press
665 Gerrard Street East
Toronto, Ontario, Canada M4M 1Y2
416-694-3348 / info@ecwpress.com

Editor for the Press: Michael Holmes
Cover design: Caroline Suzuki and Jessica Albert

LIBRARY AND ARCHIVES CANADA CATALOGUING IN PUBLICATION

Title: Winning golf : the mental game : (creating the focus, feeling, and confidence to play consistently well) / Dr. Saul L. Miller, sport and performance psychologist.

Names: Miller, Saul L., author.

Identifiers: Canadiana (print) 20220228620 | Canadiana (ebook) 20220228639

ISBN 978-1-77041-685-7 (softcover)
ISBN 978-1-77852-041-9 (ePub)
ISBN 978-1-77852-042-6 (PDF)
ISBN 978-1-77852-043-3 (Kindle)

Subjects: LCSH: Golf—Psychological aspects. | LCSH: Golfers—Psychology. | LCSH: Golf—Training.

Classification: LCC GV979.P75 M55 2022 | DDC 796.35201/9—dc23

This book is funded in part by the Government of Canada. *Ce livre est financé en partie par le gouvernement du Canada.* We also acknowledge the support of the Government of Ontario through the Ontario Book Publishing Tax Credit, and through Ontario Creates.

PRINTED AND BOUND IN CANADA   PRINTING: MARQUIS   5 4 3 2 1

To those seeking more success and
enjoyment playing golf,
a sport they love.

CONTENTS

SECTION ONE
INTRODUCTION

"A strong mind is one of the key components that
separates the great from the good."

— GARY PLAYER

CHAPTER ONE

Mapping Out the
Mental Game

"Success in golf depends less on strength of body than
upon strength of mind." – Arnold Palmer

Excellence in any sport is the result of the successful integration of
physical, technical, and mental factors. While most athletes and coaches
would agree that success on the golf course is at least 50 percent "mental," there remains a disproportionate emphasis on training the physical
and technical aspects of the game, while mental training is underrated.

But not by winners. As Jim Flick, one of golf's most prolific and
influential instructors, stated, "I've found that the player with the best
mind trumps the player with the best swing."[1]

The way I see it, the mind is a supercomputer, capable of processing
tens of thousands of thoughts, images, and feelings every day, and it's
always on. Most golfers I work with are healthy people, with sound,
high-functioning minds. As such, they are capable of running positive,
empowering mental programs. My job as a sport psychologist is to show
my clients how to develop and run high-performance programs and
how to eliminate negative, anxious, and limiting thoughts and feelings.
That's what *Winning Golf* is all about.

Max Homa put it this way: "I really enjoy working really, really hard. That's kind of my MO. And I realized that I wasn't spending enough time working on my brain. And that can get to you out here. It's a grind. We have an awesome job, but it's very lonely in your brain at times on the golf course. You have bad shots and you start kicking yourself. . . . If I'm going to work as hard as I do on the range, on the chipping green, on the putting green I need to be putting that time on myself. And that's been cool because now I feel like I'm just walking around enjoying my opportunity to compete."[2]

MANAGING EXCELLENCE

There are three key operating principles for managing excellence that apply to everything in life — including golf.

The first principle, already stated, is that the mind is like an amazing supercomputer. It's *your* supercomputer. You are able to control the flow of thoughts and feelings streaming through your mind and body. You are in charge. If what you are thinking and feeling is not positive, if it does not give you power or pleasure, change the program. Being attentive and committed to running positive programs on your mental computer is a matter of choice, and it is a critically important part of developing a winning mindset. With training and practice you will be able to do that.

The second principle is that you get more of what you focus on. The mental principle of *lateral inhibition* states that whatever we focus on becomes magnified in our perceptual field while all other stimuli are minimized. So, if what you are experiencing is something that is positive and empowering, something that gives you energy and inspires you, that programming will energize and support your performance and enjoyment on the golf course, and in life. In contrast, if you are experiencing doubt and anxious, negative, frustrating thoughts and/or tense, uncomfortable feelings, these mental programs can inevitably lead to your experiencing more tension, stress, and unease. A golfer who is thinking "Don't mess up" increases the probability that he or she will.

Sounds pretty straightforward, right? So, you may ask, "Why don't we create positive thoughts and feelings all the time?"

The third principle relates to the way our nervous systems work in that our feelings affect our thoughts, and our thoughts affect our feelings. Every time you have a tense or anxious feeling, automatically a tensing or anxious thought goes with it. The feelings and thoughts that limit most golfers have to do with difficulty, fear, and frustration. These thoughts and feelings can undermine confidence and create a sense of uncertainty in relation to the challenging task at hand.

FEELING	THOUGHT
Fear	"Don't mis-hit," "Don't mess up," "Don't ___"
Frustration	"It's not happening," "No way," "Not again," "What's the use"

The problem is these kinds of negative feelings and thoughts can produce more "limiting feelings" and "limiting thinking," creating a negative loop that's like a trap. That's how a slump develops: negative feelings feed and produce negative thoughts that create and produce more negative feelings.

SLUMP DYNAMICS

Negative feelings	Negative thoughts
Tension and fear	"Be careful," "Don't mess up"

CREATING A WINNING MENTAL GAME

In the 40 years I have consulted as a sport psychologist, I have observed three keys to creating a winning mental game: **Right Feeling, Right**

Focus, and **Right Attitude.** The three keys are interrelated and are the cornerstones of building mental strength.

Right Feeling

This means creating and maintaining the feelings/emotions that will help you to perform at your best. For some golfers that means feeling smooth, fluid, powerful, and energized. For others, it's feeling more composed, confident, centered, and in control. Right feeling also means a positive and "quiet" mind and not being distracted or limited by thoughts and feelings of doubt, uncertainty, frustration, and pressure. *Conscious Breathing* (discussed in Chapters 3 and 4) is a key to creating and maintaining right feelings.

Right Focus

Plain and simple, it's knowing who you are, what your goals are, and having a plan to achieve success, both in regard to the next shot — and in the bigger picture. Right focus is about supporting your goals with positive self-talk and high-performance imagery. It's creating a positive, healthy, high-performance mindset. We get more of what we think about. (Right Focus is outlined in Chapters 5 and 6.)

Right Attitude

Attitude is a matter of choice. A winning golf attitude is characterized by commitment, confidence, and a sense of deserving to express your ability. It is also infused with a love of golf and the never-ending challenge the sport provides. Having an attitude that incorporates all of the above is required to persevere and excel. (Right Attitude is explored in Chapters 8, 9, and 10.)

Right Golf

Combining right feeling, right focus, and right attitude leads to some truly exceptional rounds (Chapter 7).

We cover these three keys in the three sections that follow. But before we move on, let's briefly discuss the importance of goal setting and explore *your* goals. What is it that *you* want to achieve or accomplish?

WHAT ARE YOUR GOALS?

Goal setting is a driver that powers focus and action. I'm a big believer in goal setting. It's important to know what you want to achieve and to have a plan to get you there. There's a saying: a goal without a plan is just a wish. So, if you are serious about improving your golf game, set clear, meaningful goals. Put together a detailed plan with long-term, intermediate, and short-term goals, and understand that how you talk to yourself as you work toward your goals is also very important. Positive thoughts support the drive to excel and achieve. Goal setting is like planting a seed in your consciousness. Positive thinking nurtures that seed and supports it, developing into something special. Negative thinking destroys it and undermines achievement. And practice makes your goals a reality. As Greg Norman said, "Setting goals for your game is an art. The trick is setting them at the right level, neither too high or too low. A good goal should be lofty enough to inspire hard work, yet realistic enough to provide solid hope of attainment."[3]

Danielle Kang, 2020 winner of the Vare Trophy for the lowest scoring average on the LPGA Tour, sets short-term and long-term goals for each year and reviews and writes down what she is thankful for from the previous season. One of her goals for 2021 was to feel more confident over her putts. Danielle said, "I want to hit more pure putts. I want to hit better putts. I don't want to feel stressed when I putt and that's something that has really been stressing me."[4]

Create "SMART" golf goals. That is, golf goals that are **S**pecific, **M**easurable, **A**ttainable, **R**elevant, and **T**imely.

Specific: An 8 handicap, putting average of 28/round, and an NCAA scholarship are all examples of specific goals.

Measurable: The three goals above are all measurable. Setting a goal such as "improve my swing" is not.

Attainable: An 8 handicap is attainable if you have been playing as a 14 and you are prepared to put in the time and effort.

Relevant: The goals should be meaningful to you and make a positive difference in your game.

Timely: Set a specific and sensible timeline for achieving your golf goal(s).

If you are really committed to improving your game, write your golf goals down (it keeps them from being forgotten) and read them to yourself periodically.

Long-Term Goals: Set meaningful long-term goals. The most energizing goals are those that really mean something to the athlete. When I asked a very motivated, talented 15-year-old golfer what his ultimate goal was, he replied, "I want to get an NCAA golf scholarship and then, after that, turn pro." I replied, "Those are certainly impressive and challenging goals. What do you have to do to make it happen?"

Challenging, meaningful goals drive athletes to do the fitness training for greater power and endurance, the technical work for skill development and precision, and the mental-strength training to become more calm, focused, confident, and mentally tough.

Intermediate Goals: I recommend setting goals for the season, or even the month. Define the specifics of what you want to achieve in that period, set the training and competition plan to make it happen — and *do the work*.

Be specific. Think process, not simply result. That is, think of the specific behaviors you want to improve and the specific behaviors you want to eliminate to achieve the desired result. It may be very helpful to talk with your coach(es) to create your intermediate goal plan.

Short-Term Goals: It's very beneficial to set short-term goals, whether it's for your next workout or your next event. Again, be specific and process-oriented. Never underestimate the importance of settings goals and implementing them with a practice plan to develop and improve power, skill, and performance. It's important to work on both your strengths and weaknesses. Work on strengths to build and maintain your positive edge and grow your confidence. Work on weaknesses until they are no longer deficiencies. There's considerable evidence that the best way to grow an athlete's ability is with "deliberate practice," that is, with focused practice which pushes the athlete to improve specific skills (as opposed to practice that just goes over the same things you work on day after day).

Two golfing greats underline the importance of practice:

"It's a funny thing. The harder I practice,
the luckier I get." – Arnold Palmer

"The harder you practice, the luckier
you get." – Gary Player

Your goals are *your* goals. You can discuss them with a coach, or you can keep them private. What is key is that your goals are clearly defined, that there is an activity plan to achieve them, and that you do the everyday work to make them a reality.

TRAINING EXERCISES:

There are four questions:

1. What is your ultimate, long-term goal? (NCAA scholarship? Going pro? Breaking 80, 70, or lowering your handicap by 10 points?)

2. What are your intermediate goals? Goals for this season? Or, for the next three months?

3. What is your short-term goal for the next workout, or for the next competition?

4. What are you prepared to do to make that short-term goal a reality?

CHAPTER TWO

The Problem

"The mind messes up more shots than the body."
– Tommy Bolt

"What separates the great players from the
good ones is not so much ability as brain power and
emotional equilibrium."[1] – Arnold Palmer

Golf is a game of fluidity, power, precision, and consistency. Overwhelmingly, the coaching and training that golfers experience focuses on swing mechanics, with a lot of input on how to coordinate a complex combination of moving parts. And yet it is well understood that motion begins in the mind. To have a smooth, full, fluid, and effortless swing requires the mind to be relatively quiet.

COMMON GOLFING PROBLEMS

Many of the common problems golfers experience relate both to their faulty swing mechanics AND to their NOT having "right feeling" or "right focus." Let's look at eight of the most common problems golfers face and the source of these problems.

Swinging Too Hard

This is an example of trying too hard. It usually involves using too much upper body in an effort to muscle the ball. Ernie Els, a South African PGA Tour winner has said, "Your longest drives will come when you feel you're swinging 75 %."[2] And then there's the golfer's prayer: "Give me the strength to swing easy."

Swinging Too Quickly

Good tempo is key. Nick Faldo, another PGA Tour winner, has said, "Tempo is the glue that sticks all of the elements of the golf swing together."[3] Swinging too quickly (and too hard) upsets tempo. It involves being too fast on the backswing. Swinging fast is often an expression of nervousness, impatience, and, again, trying too hard.

Squeezing the Club

Holding the club in a death grip is another sign of anxiety. Whether it's golf, tennis, baseball, or hockey, athletes squeezing their equipment (club, racket, bat, or hockey stick) are expressing their nervousness and lack of confidence. And squeezing is a behavior that reduces touch, flow, and effectiveness. PGA legend Sam Snead makes the point in saying, "If a lot of people gripped a knife and fork like they grip a golf club, they'd starve to death."[4]

Lifting the Head

To maintain a complete swing with optimal tempo and balance, keep your head still and down on the strike spot until you've hit through the ball. The uncertain golfer lifts or pulls their head out and up in order to see where the ball is going. Trust your swing and the ball will go where it's supposed to. In the words of Jack Nicklaus, "Keeping the head still is golf's one universal, unarguable fundamental."[5]

Marty, an enthusiastic golfer with a great sense of humor told his golf pro that he'd found something to dramatically improve his golf game, and it had nothing to do with all the golf lessons he'd received. "It's something I discovered on my own," he said proudly. "Now that I'm swinging more easily, keeping my head still and my eye on the ball until contact, I'm playing much better golf." And he added, with a grin, "I want a refund of the thousands of dollars I paid you for my lessons."[6]

Practicing Overcontrol

Trying to steer or lift the ball is a symptom of uncertainty, anxiety, or doubt. Again, it's not trusting the swing to deliver the desired result.

Negativity

Having a negative thought or image — "don't miss," "don't slice," "don't hit it in the trees, sand, or water" — is another sign of anxiety and a lack of confidence. It's been said that having positive thoughts doesn't guarantee a positive result but a negative thought or belief almost always guarantees failure. Be positive. See and feel the shot you want to make. Billy Casper, PGA Tour Champion, said the same, "Try to think about where you want to put the ball, not where you don't want it to go."[7]

Thinking Too Much

The desire to be at your best and to score, the cost of each errant shot, the varying course challenges, your playing partners and swing mechanics (especially swing mechanics) are just a few of the subjects that can clutter a golfer's mind and interfere with performance. As Adam Hadwin stated, "You start thinking . . . and the next thing you know you are kind of missing everything."[8]

Forgetting to Enjoy the Game

Stuart Appleby, Australian PGA champion, was asked if he had any advice for an amateur playing in a Pro-Am. Stuart commented that Pro-Ams and social golf gatherings in which amateurs play with professionals of much higher skill levels can be anxiety-producing. His advice? "Get back to the basics of the game, keeping it fun. Try to enjoy it. And those principles really boil down to what professionals need to do most of the time as well. Because we can also become head cases of over-information . . . so just get out and enjoy the game. You are outdoors. Try and make it as simple as that."[9]

That's the key: enjoy the sport. As Lydia Ko commented, "I think when I'm having fun and being happy, I play the best golf. I think that's because there's less things going through my mind . . . I think it's not just myself but in general, when people are having fun they perform at their best. But it's a balance between having fun and being focused."[10]

What's common to all of the above problems is a state of angst, tension, and unease. The underlying emotion is **FEAR** and fear's many faces: anxiety, uncertainty, doubt, lack of confidence. Fear causes a subtle tension or tightening that interferes with coordination and fluidity, or flow. Combine fear with an intense desire to excel and the result is that the golfer tries too hard, swings too hard and/or too quick. Too often, the player tries to control the shot, tightens up, squeezes the club, and thinks "don't mess this up." All of which reduce the probability of experiencing the desired result.

"Of all the hazards, fear is the worst."
– Sam Snead

Most performance problems in sports are the result of a disconnect between mind and body and the ensuing feelings of unease that are created when thoughts and feelings are not in synch. Neurologically, our forebrain consists of two halves: the left and right cerebral cortices. Brain wave frequencies for the two halves differ. The left cerebral cortex processes more logical, analytic, and technical information, and is the source of beta brain waves which have frequencies of 13 to 40 cycles per second. The right cerebral cortex deals more with spatial awareness, movement, and coordination. It is the source of alpha brain waves which have slower frequencies of seven to 13 cycles per second.

Golfing success requires smooth, integrated functioning between the left and right cerebral hemispheres, between feeling and focus, focus and feeling. It's about knowing what to do and doing it. It's about the left brain thinking clearly, *but not too much*. It's about the right brain managing feelings, movement, and spatial awareness, and not letting overthinking and strong emotions skew focus. Optimal performance occurs when the two halves of the brain perform in a coordinated and integrated fashion. When people are anxious, when they are overthinking, when they are trying too hard, high beta frequencies predominate, increasing tension. Feelings of balance, flow, and spatial awareness are diminished. The ensuing anxious tensing and tightening create a state of unease which can lead to a loss of touch and rhythm, resulting in missed shots and even "choking."

The opposite of this tension, fear, and unease is *ease*. And the solution for many golf problems is learning how to bring that ease and flow to striking the ball. It's learning how to experience right feeling and right focus in the face of the pressure-filled competitive challenge that golf represents. If you feel focused and at ease, you are relaxed but ready. And when I say relax, I'm suggesting golfers do exactly what the word represents. "Re-lax" comes from the Latin *laxus*, meaning "loose," so "relax" implies regaining a natural feeling of looseness and flow. In golf, that means not squeezing or choking your club. Feel the club. Trust and feel the swing. Combine focus and power with ease and flow.

> "The most important thing is not that my short game looks good, but that it feels good, because at the end of the day what you need is to feel it." – Sergio Garcia

One of my clients once told me, "I played virtually all the major sports of the day, and at one time was a club champion golfer. It's not surprising to me that the same self-defeating mental factors that hinder optimum performance — lack of confidence, hyperattention to mechanics, trying too hard, overthinking, negativity, and tension — apply across the board to all sports. No sport, however, manifests these tendencies more than golf. Perhaps it's because golf is a very mental sport demanding precision and consistency. And because the golfer is alone and solely responsible for the result." [11]

UPPER BODY-LOWER BODY IMBALANCE

Former PGA Tour golfer, golf commentator, and innovative golf coach, Jim Nelford, pointed out another source of golfers' anxiety. Jim believes that the top-loaded, hypertechnical way many golfers are taught to approach the swing produces anxiety. He explained that in most sports, power is naturally generated from movement initiated in the lower body. Consider a pitcher in baseball. The pitcher's power comes from lower body movement; from rotating hips and leg drive, the arm follows. Similarly, a hitter gets power with lower body–initiated movement, stepping into the pitch rotating hips, with the arms (and bat) following. Movement of the body's major muscle groups, the legs and hips, is the primary source of power for almost all athletes (whether it's hitting a baseball, tennis ball, shooting a hockey puck, or throwing a football). In contrast, many golfers are taught to swing while keeping the lower body relatively still. Action is initiated in the upper body by taking the club way back and up and twisting into an uncomfortable, *uptight* position — a position that, by its very nature, creates physical and psychological stress. Adding that stress to the stress of trying to excel, Jim believes, can push a golfer's brain into high beta, setting them up to play with more anxiety. His recommendation to many uptight golfers is to calm down and come down (be centered in the lower body) with their swing.[12]

Decades ago, celebrated veteran golf instructor Jim Flick expressed his concern about too many golfers becoming overly focused on creating the perfect swing. "We've let the game be taken over by science," he said. "Golf is an art form. The golf swing is an athletic movement. Becoming mechanical and robotic is the worst thing you can do."[13]

As I've noted, uncomfortable feelings and anxious thoughts produce a surge of beta waves, which causes anxiety, overthinking, and making adjustments to unnatural swing mechanics. Throughout this book I will describe psychological techniques that will help you to play golf with focus, balance, flow, and ease. If you sense you're playing uptight, it's well worth considering creating a swing dynamic that is more natural, balanced, and consistent with the movement patterns of most sports.

MENTAL CHATTER

Some pro golfers have gone to extremes to tune out the angst and chatter in an attempt to bring more ease to their process. Here is one example: Following the release of my book *Performing Under Pressure: Gaining the Mental Edge in Business and Sport*, I was being interviewed on the radio and discussing some of the techniques described in the book and how they could enhance performance. The host of the show mentioned that he had recently interviewed Dick Zokol, who listened to a Walkman while he played to tune out any nervous and negative mental chatter. He asked what I thought about that approach. I replied, "It's not for me to be critical about what is working for him." (Note: the PGA has since made it illegal to use similar devices while playing.) Legal or not, I thought it was an unnecessary band-aid. If one learned how to create right feeling and right focus, no external input would be needed. I explained that the key to right feeling and focus involved conscious breathing and developing a quiet mind. Off the air, the radio host asked me if I would be interested in consulting with the golfer in question. I said I would, and a meeting was arranged.

I met with Dick shortly thereafter. He presented as a very capable, intelligent professional golfer. He had experienced a highly successful NCAA career and was a collegiate All-American. As a pro, he had a number of top PGA Tour finishes. Not only did he listen to music on the course to help him quiet his mind (to experience less high beta) and feel more relaxed, he explained that he also developed a very unusual pre-swing routine to control his angst. Using a heart monitor, he had observed that before he hit a ball, especially off the tee, his heart rate would accelerate dramatically. He also discovered that if, just before he hit the ball, he strongly and forcibly exhaled (making a loud "whew" sound), it sharply lowered his heart rate for a few seconds. He would then be still for a moment and before his heart rate could rise again he would swing the club. So, the routine he developed was to align to the target, waggle his club up and down, let the tension and heart rate build, blow off the angst ("whew!"), be still for a moment . . . then swing.

My reaction to both the use of the music and his unusual pre-swing routine was, again, "If that works, fine." However, I was fairly certain if we worked with his breathing and with some positive self-talk and imagery, his mind would become quieter and his game could be simpler, more enjoyable, and more effective. After that, we spent a couple of sessions working with these core elements.

It's important both to work in practice to develop good swing mechanics and to learn to control your mind, so that on the golf course you can tune out the nervous "trying" and critical thinking, and instead trust and feel your smooth, full swing when striking the ball.

> "It's harder to groove your mind than your
> golf swing."[14] — Barry McDonnell

The following article describes an experience I had consulting with the Mississippi State University golf team when I was teaching there several decades ago. It involved the application of the techniques outlined in this book, specifically to the problems discussed in this chapter. The results were very positive.

"Shrink" Shrinks MSU Golf Scores
by Verenda Smith
The Clarion-Ledger (Jackson, MS) April 26, 1981

At first, Gary Meredith's golfers didn't think much of the idea of "going to see a shrink." "I had almost to take them by the hand and go over there with them for the first few visits," Meredith recalled. "They were saying, 'Hey, there's nothing wrong with me, what do I need a shrink for?'" Because they were losers.

Meredith was coaching a team at Mississippi State that simply never got anywhere. In day-in, day-out competition, the Bulldogs would often find themselves outclassed. They couldn't even kick themselves out of the dregs of the Southeastern Conference, much less stand toe-to-toe with quality national competition. Meredith is an open-minded man, and he knew of modern technical changes he could make to better teach and train his golfers. Among other things the Bulldogs began weight-lifting and became a highly conditioned squad. But all the little things like corrected grips, added strength and altered swings won't turn around a team that's accustomed to the idea of being defeated, beaten by both the course and by the opposing teams. That's when Meredith dragged his players in for a little chat with Saul Miller.

Miller is a psychologist at State, a man interested in the effect the mind can have on athletes' performances. They don't call them "shrinks" anymore. And it didn't take long for the players to figure out that his ideas just might lower their scores. They soon began to show up at his office without being towed by Meredith. Not many weeks later Miller was sitting in a wrought iron chair under a shade tree over-looking the golf course at the Country Club of Jackson, talking to the players who dashed up to discuss their mental success on the course that day, and then would trot off to discuss their pars and bogeys with their "other" coach Meredith.

"Miller helped this team to the degree of turning them from losers to winners," Meredith said. "That's the hard thing for me. If a team was already a winner, he could help it some, but the degree of help wouldn't be as outstanding. . . . We're still climbing. We're not a championship team yet. But you can put all the other things together, and if you don't have it up here," he said as he tapped his head. "Then you have got a loser."[15]

In the next nine chapters we will explore how to bring more ease, flow, and power to the moment and how to create the "right" feeling and focus that will enhance your golfing performance and pleasure.

SECTION TWO
RIGHT FEELING

"Golf is a game of emotion and adjustment. If you are not aware of what is happening in your mind and your body when you are playing you will never be able to be the very best you can be." – Jack Nicklaus

"Self-doubt is because you're into the result and not into the process of what you are doing. You are too result-oriented. You've got to create fun in what you are doing. It's the fun of the challenge. It's still focused. It's still driven. But you are not obsessed by the result. You are in the moment. . . . As a performer if you go on and try too hard, you're burdened with tightness – 'I want to do this so badly it hurts . . .' then you are not going to perform. . . . It's never life or death. When it's too important for me, that's when it's the worst."[1] – Paul McGinley

In the next section (Chapters 3 and 4), we will emphasize the importance of creating "right feelings" — specifically, feelings of power and calm — and describe how to use conscious breathing to accomplish that. Golfing success is about managing feelings and focus. Remember, your feelings affect your thoughts. You can't maintain positive performance focus without managing or eliminating feelings of anxiety, frustration, and fatigue.

The three keys to managing your mental game are knowing:

1. You are capable of running positive programs on your mental supercomputer. If you don't like what you are thinking or feeling, change the program. You're the boss.

2. Your feelings affect your thinking, and your thinking affects your feelings. Calm, powerful feelings lead to positive, confident thoughts. Tense, anxious, frustrated feelings lead to negative thinking, poor performance . . . and more negative feelings. Maintain a positive focus. Focusing on negatives — for example, how bad something is — tends to make the situation worse.

3. Attitude is a matter of choice. Whenever you are confronted by a challenging, difficult situation, you always have a choice: either you *use it* . . . or it can use you. Playing winning golf is about *using it*, about creating right focus and right feelings.

CHAPTER THREE

Managing Emotions –
Conscious Breathing

"Best golf tip ever: don't forget to breathe."[1]
– Tom Blanckaert

Golf is an exacting sport that demands consistency. To compete successfully, you must be able to manage your emotions and create right feelings. That means not only being able to energize, focus, and *attack* the course, but also being *smooth* — that is, calm and composed. Many golfers struggle with maintaining the right attack/smooth balance. The exact balance point varies depending on a golfer's personality, talent, experience, and, in some cases, the situation.

The relationship between athletic performance and emotional intensity is depicted in figure 3.1. As emotional intensity increases, performance improves until it peaks at an optimal level. Thereafter, increases in intensity cause an athlete to be too pumped, too intense, too tight (over-aroused), and performance decreases.

Most golfers I've consulted with think they are at their best in the range of 6 to 7.5. If your emotional intensity is very low (2 or 3), you have to pick it up, draw in power, and then attack mentally. A

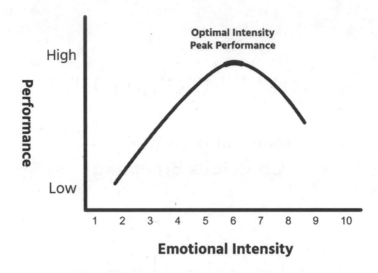

Figure 3.1. The relationship between performance and emotional intensity.

more common problem is having emotional intensity that is above your optimal level, which leads to trying too hard, tensing, and feeling tight. In that case, breathing can help you calm your emotions. For more intensity, the key word is "attack." For more calm, the key word is "smooth." Remember, you're the boss. You have the response-ability to control your feelings.

After winning the men's individual golf event at the 2020 Olympics (held in the summer of 2021), Xander Schauffele commented, "I felt that most part of the day I stayed very calm. I usually look calm but there's something terrible happening inside and I was able to learn from those moments. I've lost (tournaments) coming down the stretch where I hit a bad shot or a bad wedge or a bad putt and sort of lose my cool. But today . . . I'm just happy I could fall back on parts of my game to pull me through. . . . I've never done that before. It's a first for me to have the lead and be able to cap it off."[2]

Two questions I'm frequently asked are, how do I know what number I am on the performance arousal scale, and what should I be? Everyone is different. Take some time to tune in and become aware of how you feel when you are performing at your best. On the golf course, if you are experiencing an emotional intensity that is higher than your optimal level, learn to use your breathing and thinking to adjust.

It's a skill you'll acquire by practicing the exercises described throughout this book. And, it's a skill that will enable you to develop emotional control for competitive mastery. If a golfer feels nervous and stressed, consistency and enjoyment suffer. Learning to manage your emotions will help you to stay healthy, energized, and positively focused. And conscious breathing is the first step to taking back control.

> "For this game you need above all things
> to be in a tranquil frame of mind."
> – Harry Vardon

Two things happen when you focus on your breathing. First, conscious breathing helps you to be in the present moment. When athletes feel anxious and worried, it's usually about the future (e.g., "What'll happen if I perform poorly, miss the shot, embarrass myself . . ."). Frustration, on the other hand, lives in the past, when athletes become preoccupied with mistakes made and opportunities squandered.

The power is in the present. *Now* **is where the action is.** Focusing on breathing brings your conscious mind into the "here-and-now" present. If you find yourself stuck worrying about the past or the future, take a breath and bring your attention back to this breath . . . back to the now.

On this point, Paul Azinger, a multiple-time PGA Tour winner said, "Staying in the present is the key to any golfer's game. Once you start thinking about a shot you just messed up or what you have to do on the next nine to catch somebody, you're lost."[3]

Immediately after winning the British Open, Collin Morikawa was asked, "Everyone remarks on how calm, collected, and cool you look on the golf course on what was presumably a tense pressure situation. Are you that calm and collected or are you jumping up and down inside? And, if you are so calm, how do you manage to feel that way?"

Morikawa responded, "Well, I'm glad I look calm because the nerves are definitely up there. But you channel these nerves into excitement and energy and it puts you away from a fear factor into, this is something I want. That's how I look at it. . . . You can't worry about the score. I have to think about every shot. Can I execute every shot to the best of my ability? Some we did, some we didn't, and then you move on. I can't control what's going to happen or what has happened. So, I really look at that as, focus on every shot. How do I see what is the best shot possible and try and do my best from there."[4]

Annika Sorenstam, an LPGA Tour Champion, said something very similar: "I've learned how to control emotions. I've learned how to just focus on the upcoming shot, play the shot in the now. It's the most important shot . . . not what you did 10 minutes ago and not what you are going to do 10 minutes from now. It's this particular shot. . . . I like to say that the mental aspect of my game has always been my strong suit."[5]

Breathing can keep you focused in the present, in the now. It's always "this breath."

Second, conscious breathing integrates mind and body. Most performance problems are the result of a disconnect between thoughts (your mind) and feelings (your body): mind and body are not in synch. It's as though these two parts are operating at different speeds. Frequently, the mind seems to be racing, leaving the body behind. Conscious breathing allows you to integrate your thoughts and feelings.

As explained in the last chapter, left and right cerebral cortices of our brains differ. The left cerebral cortex which processes more analytic and technical information, like shot analysis and complex swing mechanics, is the source of beta brain frequencies. The right half of the brain deals more with feeling, spatial awareness, movement, and coordination. It is the source of alpha brain wave frequencies.

Because golfing success requires smooth, integrated functioning between the left and right cerebral hemispheres, between feeling and focus, optimal performance occurs when these two halves of the brain perform in a coordinated and integrated fashion. Again, when a golfer is anxious and overthinking, high beta frequencies predominate and flow, coordination, and spatial awareness are diminished. The anxiety, tension, and tightening create a loss of touch and rhythm, resulting in missed shots and poor play.

Smooth conscious breathing is one of the simplest and most effective ways to facilitate that coordination and contribute to a high-performance state. *Winning Golf* is about having focus, power, and emotional control. Conscious breathing is a key to all three.

> "When I learned how to breathe, I learned
> how to win." – Tom Watson

There is considerable scientific evidence that slow, relaxed breathing techniques act to enhance autonomic, cerebral, and psychophysical flexibility, promoting greater emotional control and psychological well-being.[6]

Breathing is a part of several performance-enhancement programs. Recently, one program that emerged with a strong breathing component is Neuropeak Pro, who list Bryson DeChambeau as one of their clients. They state, "Breathing is the foundation of all of our programs. That's because our breath has the power to engage our sympathetic and parasympathetic nervous systems. The problem is, many of us are actually breathing in a way that isn't beneficial to our bodies."[7]

I asked LPGA legend Nancy Lopez if she ever used breathing to calm herself down on the golf course. Nancy replied, "Yes I did. I took deep breaths and let it flow through my body. I felt that I was pretty good at taking a deep breath when I needed it. I think that's important. When I'm teaching now, I tell people when they're under pressure it's okay to take a deep breath. Some people think when they take that deep breath, they're showing weakness, and they don't do it, so no one will see them doing it. I know when you can take some really good deep breaths, there is a release. It's a good feeling and it definitely helps."[8]

CONSCIOUS BREATHING . . . GENERATING POSITIVE FEELINGS AND POSITIVE RESULTS

Here is a simple breathing process that is basic to generating right feelings and managing emotions. It's one of the most important performance-enhancing techniques I use. And it is applicable to almost everything we do in life.

The three keys to conscious breathing are **Rhythm**, **Inspiration** (the inbreath), and **Direction**. In these exercises and in life, whenever possible, I recommend you breathe slowly and smoothly . . . and through the nose. It is the most efficient way to absorb oxygen.

After reading through the process, I suggest you record the exercise on your phone or iPad.

That way you can play it back to yourself, relax, and really experience the process without having to read it.

RHYTHM

Perhaps the most important part of breathing is simply tuning in to the rhythm of your breath.

To get into your breathing rhythm, sit back and relax.
And feel the inbreath come in . . .
And feel the outbreath go out . . .

Again, feel the inbreath come in . . .
And feel the outbreath go out . . .

The key to rhythm is time.
Give yourself time for the inbreath to come all the way in . . .
Give yourself time for the outbreath to flow all the way out . . .

Now place a hand on your abdomen and one on your chest.
Notice as you breathe in . . . the abdomen and chest rise.
As you breathe out . . . they fall.

The breath is like waves in the ocean.
You can always find the waves.
And the waves will help you to feel calm and strong.

Sit back, relax, give yourself time to feel the inbreath, the
in-wave flowing in . . .
Give yourself time to feel the outbreath, the out-wave flowing
out . . .
It's very simple. There's power in simplicity.

Now imagine competing. . . . You are totally into it. When
there is a break in the action, the first thing we do is catch our
breath. That is, we instinctively slip back into the waves and our
natural breathing rhythm.

Experience the subtle power in connecting to your natural
rhythm. It's a way to take control.

INSPIRATION

Once you have tuned in to your breathing rhythm, the second thing to focus on is the inbreath, the *inspiration*.

"Inspiration" means to take in spirit.

Your breathing is a source of energy and spirit.

Again, tune in to your breathing.

Experience a nice smooth rhythm.

Give yourself time for the inbreath to come all the way in . . .

Give yourself time for the outbreath to flow all the way out . . .

Now, imagine that you are surrounded with unlimited energy.

As you breathe in, feel yourself drawing some of that energy to you . . .

It's there for you wherever you may be.

Again, relax and breathe . . .

And consciously draw in energy and power with each inbreath you take . . .

You have a personal connection to an unlimited supply of energy.

DIRECTION

Experience a nice smooth breathing rhythm . . .

Feel yourself breathing in energy . . .

Now on the outbreath, allow yourself to imagine energy flowing down . . .

Through your shoulders, arms, and into the palms of your hands . . .

One more time, feel yourself drawing in, breathing in energy.
Again, allow yourself to imagine energy flowing down your
arms . . .
Into your hands . . . and out into the shaft and head of the
club . . .
Feel the club as an extension of you.

Now, imagine yourself breathing in energy.
This time, on the outbreath, allow energy to flow down your
legs and into your feet . . .

Again, feel yourself breathing in energy.
And on the outbreath, allow that energy to flow down your legs
and into the soles of your feet . . .
Feel the energy in the soles of your feet . . .
Feel that you have a solid base and good balance . . .

It's always a smooth breathing rhythm . . . like waves in the ocean.
Breathing in energy and sending it out . . .
Allowing it to flow down the arms, the hands, and into the golf
club . . . strong hands.
Down the legs and feet . . . good balance . . . solid base . . .

Okay, once again experience a smooth breathing rhythm . . .
breathing in energy.
This time as you breathe out, imagine energy flowing up your
spinal column, up into your head and eyes.
Now, close your eyes and allow the place behind your eyes to
relax.
As you relax and breathe . . . feel energy flowing to you . . . and
through you . . .
Out to your hands, feet, and eyes, like a 5-pointed star . . .

Figure 3.2. The flow of energy through eyes, hands, and feet as a 5-pointed star.

As you relax and breathe . . . know that you are a good golfer.
Think of your strengths . . . three to four reasons why you are good.
Imagine yourself making some of your finest golfing strokes . . . with excellent form and precision.
See it . . . Feel it . . .

For the next four to five minutes, simply relax and breathe.

"Under pressure, one of the most important
things I have to remember is to breathe."
– Curtis Strange

Any questions? When I was working with a university golf team, one golfer raised a question that several golfers had previously asked. "This feels relaxing enough," he said. "But, frankly, I don't see how it's going to help me when I'm in an NCAA tournament, on the fifth hole, with a dozen more holes to play. What does this relaxed breathing stuff really have to do with competitive golf?"

As I said earlier, success in golf — and life — is about learning how to manage your mind. A key to managing your mental game is being able to generate feelings of ease and power in any situation. By practicing these techniques every day in a comfortable place, when there is no stress or demand for action, you will develop the capacity under pressure to simply take a breath and feel more calm, powerful, confident, and in control.

Discussing the importance of conscious breathing with Jim Nelford, a former PGA Tour player who is now an instructor, I related the comments of Duncan Keith. Keith is an all-star hockey player who has excelled in the game for 18 seasons. One of the things he attributes to his longevity and high level of play is the work he does with breathing. Keith said, "Breathing and the power of the brain are two things in hockey or sports that don't get enough attention. I don't know why that is. The muscles and aesthetics get mentioned — everyone wants to look good — and that's important, for sure. There's meditation breathing to bring your nervous system down to more of a parasympathetic state, where you're relaxing, and you're able to recover and rest. . . . I work on my breathing and the mechanics of it a lot. I actually really started getting into proper breathing eight years ago, and have taken it to the next level in the last year especially. So that's something I'll continue working on."[9]

Jim Nelford's response to Keith's comments was, "I certainly agree about the importance of learning to be more conscious of your breathing, and how that affects the body. It is one of the major indicators of being able to switch minds. To go from 'freaking out to freaking in.' Being able to control our fear and anxiety in the game of golf is paramount." Jim added, "Learning to do it when the onus is on the player making it happen, versus the action of a ball or puck making you react, is a different kettle of fish. The awareness of where we operate from physically and mentally is even more critical in the game of golf, as we obviously have to play all of our misses. And it is out there for all to see."[10]

> "One way to break up any kind of tension is
> good deep breathing." – Byron Nelson

I suggest you practice these breathing exercises *every day*. There's scientific evidence that if you do them regularly, you will be able to manage stress and your emotions more effectively under pressure. This is important. Let me say it again: with regular practice, you will develop the capacity on the golf course to simply take a breath (or two) and be able to feel more calm, powerful, and in control.

Remember, the breath is like waves in the ocean.
And you can always find the waves.
Feel energy flowing to you and through you.
The waves can wash away anxiety, tension, and negativity.

Work with your breathing to improve your golf swing.
Experience breathing in on the back swing . . .
And breathing out on the downswing . . .

The golf ball has no energy of its own. It gets its energy from *you*. The more easily energy flows to you and through you, the more power and accuracy you will express in your swing and your game.

TRAINING EXERCISES

There are four exercises associated with this chapter. I encourage you to be diligent in your practice of these assignments.

1. For 10 to 15 minutes *every day*, do conscious breathing, directing the flow of energy (5-pointed star), positive self-talk, and positive imagery.

2. Once a day, after breathing and relaxing, spend a couple of minutes imagining energy flowing to you and through you. Now direct that energy through the club to the ball and play with smoothness and focus.

3. On the golf course, practice taking a breath and thinking "calm and strong." It will help you to feel calm and strong.

4. (Optional) Keep a journal. Record any thoughts and feelings you may have about these mental-management processes and any observations about how they impact your golfing experience. This is private, so you can be entirely honest with yourself.

CHAPTER FOUR

Changing Programs – The Release Reflex

"You can talk strategy all you want,
but what really matters is resiliency." – Hale Irwin

To be a consistent high-level performer it's important to be able to change tense, anxious, and negative thoughts and feelings into something positive. One question I'm often asked — and it's a good one — is, "What can I do when I'm really upset or frustrated to get out of that negative-feeling space?"

Hanging your head, swearing, getting angry, or being self-deprecating does nothing to improve your emotional or mental state. In fact, because we get more of what we think about, dwelling on the negative only makes it more likely that a decrease in performance will follow. Golf challenges us to be resilient and positive.

The question really is, how can I quickly and effectively change my thoughts and feelings into something positive and powerful? Or to put it a different way, what is the mechanism for changing programs on my mental computer? The answer — the release reflex — is based on the conscious breathing and the tension-release process we introduced in Chapter 3.

THE RELEASE REFLEX

The release reflex is remarkably simple. Whenever you feel tension, anxiety, negativity, or frustration, **release** it . . . **breathe** in . . . and **refocus**.

The Release Reflex is a simple 3-step process:

1. Release (tension or negativity).
2. Breathe in energy.
3. Refocus on the positive.

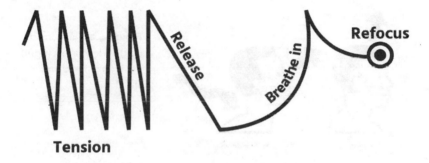

Figure 4.1. The release reflex process.

To practice the release reflex, we add to the conscious breathing process we just learned.

Once we have eliminated tension and negativity, the next step is to **refocus on a positive thought or image**.

To begin, make tight fists and feel the tension between the
fingers and in the center of the hand . . . bend the wrists in . . .
and hold for five seconds.
Now release the tension . . . and take a breath . . .
That ability to release tension and take a breath is key.
Remember, it's always release and breathe IN.

Next, raise your shoulders toward your ears . . . feel the tension, notice how it cuts down breathing . . . hold for five seconds.
Then release the tension and breathe in . . .
Again, be aware of that feeling of letting go.
It's always release and breathe in.

The neck and shoulders are a primary tension-holding area.

When people are stressing, they often pull their head back and down creating more tension.

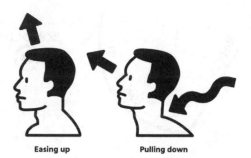

Easing up   **Pulling down**

Figure 4.2. The correct (left) and incorrect (right) position of head and shoulders.

Be aware that when you release tension in the neck and shoulders, you allow your head to move forward and up as you breathe.

This time raise the shoulders just one inch.
The tensing is almost imperceptible to others, but you can feel it, and it cuts down breathing.
Hold for five seconds . . .
Then release and breathe . . .
Again, understand **it's always release and breathe in**.

Now, imagine someone directing a punch at your head, you see it coming, and you duck.
It's a protective reflex. It's automatic.

Similarly, if you imagine someone standing right in front of you being confrontational and highly critical, a reflexive tensing occurs.

Now, this is what we've been building up to.

Whenever you experience a negative, anxious, or frustrated thought, it will automatically trigger a tensing reaction in the body.

The solution or response to that tensing reflex is, again, to

- Release the tension
- Breathe in energy
- Refocus on a positive thought or feeling

What is important to understand is that, for an instant, the release and breathe process will clear the screen on your mental computer and wipe out the tension, negativity, and anxiety you are experiencing. You should then refocus and replace the negative feeling or thought with a positive feeling or thought (e.g., "smooth" or "Yes I can").

Client comment: "I truly believe that the release reflex technique has had the most impact on my golfing career so far. I think this technique is amazing; without it my scores would be significantly higher. Whenever I am anxious, whenever I am frustrated, I know I can rely on "release-breathe-refocus." It keeps me in the present, and it resets my mind to making a good next shot."[1]

The release reflex is key to mental management.

The release reflex is the most effective way to clear the screen on your mental computer and introduce a program that is positive and powerful. Releasing involves first being aware of tension, anxiety, frustration, or negativity, and then letting it go. Remember, feelings affect thinking, and you're the boss of your feelings. You have control over them.

Lee Westwood, an English PGA star who has won tournaments on five continents, said, "It's such a psychological and mental game golf, that the smallest wrong thing at the wrong time can distract you from what you are trying to achieve."[2] That's why learning how to deal with pressure and using the release reflex to change undesirable thinking and feeling is an invaluable skill in golf and in life.

THE RELEASE REFLEX IN PRACTICE – DEALING WITH BAD SHOTS

When I asked Nancy Lopez how she dealt with a poor shot, she replied, "When you have a bad shot, you have to shake it off, take a breath, and bring an excited attitude to the next shot. If you keep the bad shot feeling, you are more likely to hit the next one poorly too. I always stepped up to the next shot with the attitude that I am going to make my best swing and hit this one great!"

She added, "Golf is an emotional game and I felt I controlled my emotions better than most players, and that was because of my dad. He made it that hitting a bad shot wasn't a big deal. I just focused on hitting the next shot great, and getting back on track . . . and not worrying about what happened on the last shot. I was just able to do that and it would calm my mind. Because, if you miss a shot or you're struggling, it's easy to start thinking about too many things and you will not have the clear mind to just hit the next ball with your best attitude and swing. There were times in that final round, on the final day, in the last group, I would see a player's body language change after she missed a shot. To me, her emotions were getting to her and I knew at that time I was going to beat her because her body language changing would prevent her from getting back into that positive state of mind. When you start to struggle you feel different and then the way you approach any shot becomes a struggle. I didn't hit every shot great so I accepted that, but I always gave a hundred percent every time I stood over a shot."[3]

Dustin Johnson was once asked, "How do you deal with bad shots? Do you have any skills, any things you work on for that?" He replied, "Yeah, I mean obviously hitting a poor shot in certain situations aggravates or frustrates me. But you know I learned early and in college too, it does no good to be upset with a shot. I mean I've already hit it. There's nothing I can do about it other than go find it and hit it again. Yeah, I'm frustrated at that instance when I hit it, but after I take a couple of steps it's done and I'm thinking about the next shot I gotta hit."[4]

If you want to control your anxious, negative thinking and tense feelings under pressure, I recommend working *every day* with conscious breathing, the release reflex, and refocusing. You do not need to be in a high-pressure environment to practice these techniques. You can do these exercises in a relaxed setting, away from the competitive golf scene. As long as you work with these techniques every day, they will be there for you when moments of pressure arise. I encourage you to practice the release reflex until it acquires enough habit strength to become a reliable way to manage your thoughts and feelings under pressure.

I often mention to clients that I know if I go to the gym and lift weights I will get stronger. However, knowing this information, understanding what's being said, is not enough. To acquire the ability to manage your emotions under pressure, you have actually to do the training, repeatedly.

Again, learning how to change your mental programs and release anxious thoughts and tense feelings is an invaluable tool for excelling in the exacting game of golf. And, it takes understanding and practice to be able to implement it in the pressure of competition. Working with conscious breathing and the release reflex can help you to do that.

"When I'm in the zone, I don't think about a shot or the wind or the distance or the gallery or anything. I just pull a club and swing." – Mark Calcavecchia

Lee Trevino put it this way: "You can't think when you swing. The more you think the worse you'll play. What's happened, unfortunately, I mean no disrespect by this, is that people who are teaching are getting too crazy with too many little movements and muscles. You can't let too many people mess with you."[5]

In his excellent *Inner Game* approach to sport, Tim Gallwey explains he is trying to accomplish two objectives. The first is increasing the athletes' potential, and the second is decreasing the interference with that potential. Gallwey has said, "Doubt, fear, trying too hard, over-control, and attachment to results all interfere with the potential the person has."[6]

Gallwey describes two mental processes, what he refers to as Self 1 and Self 2. Self 1 is a conscious, analytic voice in our heads that is supervising and too often critiquing the performance of Self 2. Self 1 is more the ego, left side of the brain. Self 2 is more the intuitive, right side of the brain. In golf, Self 2 is that instinctive, feeling, in-the-flow part of our selves — the part that is responsible for swinging the club and striking the golf ball.

Here's the problem. Fundamentally, Self 1 doesn't trust Self 2 to strike the ball well. Self 1 is critical about past errors and concerned about possible, even probable, future miscues. Self 1's lack of trust of Self 2 to play well (or we could say the conscious/left brain/ego's lack of trust to perform an effective intuitive action) leads Self 1 to provide Self 2 with instructions as to how to swing the club. Self 1's analytic and anxiety-charged mental chatter interferes with Self 2's natural ability to have a smooth, fluid, full, powerful "natural" swing. The more Self 1 doesn't trust Self 2, the more "instructive" mental chatter Self 1 broadcasts. When a golfer is relaxed and confident, there is less Self 1 chatter. Gallwey explained that when he observed and came to appreciate that Self 1 tended to be more of a hindrance than a help to Self 2, he began to look for ways to quiet Self 1.

Gallwey first wrote about managing Self 1's interference in Self 2's instinctive responsiveness in his book *The Inner Game of Tennis* in 1974. In that book Gallwey described how instructing Self 1 to think "bounce-hit" busied that part of the analytic mind and kept it from interfering with Self 2's more instinctive, natural, athletic way of hitting the tennis ball.

With golf, one suggestion Gallwey made for reducing Self 1's interference with Self 2 was to have the golfer busy Self 1 with the instruction to focus on three simple swing *feeling* points that Gallwey labels *da, da, da*. These swing feeling points are

"da" 1: when the club peaks at the backswing
"da" 2: when the club strikes the ball
"da" 3: at the end of the follow-through

Gallwey suggests that having Self 1 attend to da 1, da 2, and da 3 will "pre-occupy" Self 1 and, in so doing, will prevent Self 1 from being hyper-analytic, critical, and interfering with Self 2 playing the shot. He stresses the importance of rehearsing Self 1's "*da, da, da*" focus in practice situations on the range or putting green before trying it in competitive situations where the pressure to get a result is great and where Self 1 is more inclined to be analytic and intrusive.[7]

Using Gallwey's Self 1 and Self 2 terminology, I have found an alternative and, I believe, simpler way to remove Self 1's interference, and that is by instructing Self 1 to breathe. Prior to addressing the ball, take a complete breath. Then breathe in on the backswing as you load and breathe out as you strike the ball. Feeling the breath quiets the left brain, the source of analytic thought, and thus reduces anxiety and interference with ball striking. *To put it simply, if you are overthinking things, if you are worried, if you are tensing . . . release . . . breathe in . . . and swing smooth.*

"Your final goal is to convert your athletic
swing to pure instinct rather than conscious
thought." – David Leadbetter

Justin Thomas has said, "Swing like you don't care."[8] Swinging like you don't care and breathing is good advice. However, it's easier said than done. Some clients who have found it particularly challenging to stay smooth under pressure were those golfers coming off playing NCAA golf and trying to make it on one of the professional satellite tours. Over the years, I've consulted with many young professional athletes playing in the minor leagues in baseball and hockey who aspired to make it to the "bigs." No doubt they experienced lots of pressure. However, they all had a salary and the security of a contract. Golfers coming out of college and trying to make it on to a professional golf circuit have little security, if any. They have no salary and no contract. The "meter" is constantly running for them. Every tournament they qualify for has fees, in addition to the significant travel and living expenses they have to meet. On top of that are the intense pressures to perform, make the cut, and finish near the top of the leaderboard. All of these pressures can lead to trying too hard, overthinking, overarousal, tensing, squeezing (generating too much high beta) and underachieving. The conscious breathing work described in Chapters 3 and 4 is definitely something this doctor prescribes.

Jeff was one of these young, hopeful professionals. He had been a good collegiate golfer on a good BYU golf team. He was the darling of his golf club, and the members were supporting/sponsoring Jeff's first year of trying to make it in professional golf — and "trying" it was. Jeff explained that he found it much more challenging than playing in college. Not because the game was any different — sure the competition was better — but it was mainly because of his awareness of the "cost to perform" and the intense pressure he felt to please his sponsors.[9]

Similarly, Alexander said, "The step from high school to college golf was a big jump, but the leap from college to the professional ranks is a different ball game. You really have to elevate your mental game. You're competing against the world . . . it's a big adjustment. And it's especially tough when you know other people are funding your tournament play and they have an expectation for you to play well. It's in the back of your head and you have to do everything in your power to block that out. You have to play your game — that's what the best players do. I can't have in the back of my mind that if I don't play well my sponsor is going to be upset with me, and I'm going to be getting a phone call. I think a lot of college golfers are experiencing that fear of disappointing and not fulfilling what is expected of them. Bottom line, if I'm playing with fear, I'm not going to make it, and I should just give up right now — there's no chance for me".[10]

Golf legend Bobby Jones was quoted as saying, "Competitive golf is a game played mainly on a five-and-a-half-inch course . . . the space between your ears."[11] My sessions with players making the transition to the pro golf circuits don't focus on swing mechanics, but on learning to breathe, to release anxious thinking and feelings, and to create a clear and positive focus, power, and ease.

> "I play the best when I focus on staying in a good place mentally and keep the technique simple." – Rickie Fowler

Here's testimony from a client, a former club champion: "I believe most golfers cannot fail to elevate their performance by practicing Dr. Miller's techniques. In my particular case, after exploring these techniques, I found myself letting go and 'just doing it' instead of my usual tense focus trying to rediscover the right technique. The result was I was hitting the ball with more power, ease, and a feeling I had honestly not experienced in several decades."[12]

> "The simpler I keep things the better I play."
> – Nancy Lopez

GENERATING POWER – TURNING THE WHEEL

In the last chapter, I said that there were three things to focus on while doing conscious breathing:

1. Rhythm
2. Inspiration
3. Direction (directing energy out into your feet, hands, and eyes)

The same thing applies to another enjoyable breathing exercise, "turning the wheel."

Imagine that the breath is like a wheel.
As you breathe in, the wheel turns up.
As you breathe out, the wheel turns down, making a complete circle.
Turning the wheel generates power.
You are a power generator.

Imagine power being generated from the body's gravitational center below the navel.
Place a hand on that power center just below your navel.
Now breathe . . .
Turn the wheel and send that power out through the body.
Again, experience your breathing rhythm . . .
On the inbreath, the wheel turns up . . .
On the outbreath, the wheel turns down . . .
Go deeper into the breathing.
Feel yourself breathing in energy and sending out power, like a 5-pointed star . . .
Now imagine you are about to step up to the tee.
You want to be sharp, centered, and powerful.
Turn the wheel to generate power. Feel it in your core.

Breathe energy in and send energy out through relaxed shoulders and loose arms, into your hands . . .

Figure 4.3. Sending power throughout the body by breathing.

A winning strategy for golf *and* life is: whatever comes up, **USE IT**. In golf, "using it" means using a negative thought or tense feeling as a cue to stimulate you to turn the wheel and refocus on the positive. Everything we experience is a *stimulus*. The way in which you react to the stimuli you experience is your decision. You're the boss. Anxiety, negativity, and frustration are all stimuli. Use negativity and frustration to signal you to go deeper into your breathing, to turn the wheel, and to create feelings of ease and power that will enable you to compete and excel. In the words of Sergio Garcia, "If you worry about making bogeys, it makes the game much more difficult. You put more pressure on yourself without even noticing it. It makes a difference to take it easy when things aren't going right."[13]

Another breathing technique that some clients have found an effective way to both increase intensity and reduce anxiety and tension is something I borrowed from the martial arts. It's something to be practiced alone, in a private setting, and away from the golf course. It involves starting with some "turning the wheel" breathing and then focusing the energy generated into a series of short punches that are not directed at anyone. It's as though you are punching through a block of soft, corky wood. Each punch is accompanied by a deep-seated yell. There is a specific way to punch and yell that can be communicated with a little coaching. However, any series of six to eight short, crisp punches accompanied by a deep, core-centered yell (not throat-centered) can be energizing and at the same time can help you to blow off tension.

Practicing this technique, the classic karate yell sound of *kiai* can be used, or you can use whatever sound feels right to you. If the concept appeals to you, check it out, and *practice it* as a way to blow off tension, remembering to slip back into your smooth, natural breathing rhythm. On the golf course punching and yelling is inappropriate. To blow off tension on the course, transform the punch and yell technique you've been practicing to a hand pump and a strong exhalation, then slip back to your natural breathing rhythm.

Sleep: For many golfers, sleep is a nonissue. For others, the pressure around tournaments can contribute to significant sleep problems before a tournament (anxious anticipation) and during and after a tournament (reflective frustration as well as anxiety). Discussing his famous meltdown at the 1996 Masters, Greg Norman, who was leading by 6 strokes going into the final round said, "I'm probably the only guy in the world who thinks, 'I don't know if I can hold it.'" And when asked how his Saturday night went, he replied, "I didn't sleep a wink."[14]

A simple sleep solution is to experience the breath as waves (as in the breathing exercise described above): On the inbreath, the wave flows in; on the outbreath, the wave flows out. Understand that the waves can wash away tension, anxiety, and frustration. You can facilitate the process by counting: 1 on the in-wave/inbreath and 1 on the out-wave/outbreath. Then 2 on the in-wave and 2 on the out-wave. Then back to 1 on the in-wave and 1 on the out-wave; 2 on the in-wave and 2 on the out-wave. Keep the waves flowing and keep the count 1 and 2 as you watch the breath. When thoughts come to mind, let them go and slip back into the waves and the count. This simple process busies the active mind with something that is soothing and quieting, and facilitates sleep. It's a process I have personally found to be very beneficial.

Pain can be a part of striving for excellence in all sports, including golf. If pain is a nonissue for you, then skip the next few paragraphs. (Be aware that certain injuries require medical care, and you should seek medical attention if you are dealing with acute or chronic pain. Of course, there may be times when in order to compete you will need to play while in pain.)

Pain can be a product of overuse, especially overuse with uptight mechanics. Check out how you are using yourself and if you are unnecessarily stressing your body as you swing the club.

While running an interdisciplinary pain clinic for a number of years, I observed that *going into the pain* is an effective focusing strategy for dealing with pain. When you experience pain, you can use it as a stimulus or reminder to go deeper into your breathing. Specifically, think of your breathing rhythm. Pain can disorganize that rhythm. It can cause contraction and shorten your breath. What's essential is that you regain your rhythm, and the easiest and most powerful way to do that is with *conscious breathing*. As your breathing rhythm begins to strengthen, see if you can create a feeling of ease where the pain is located, rather than the dis-ease that lives there. Imagine sending a soothing energy into the area. You can give a color to the imagined energy depending on what you need: red or gold for warmth, or blue and green for coolness.

Again, release the tension, breathe, and send soothing energy to and through the stressed or painful area. If you try to fight or avoid the pain, you may increase tension and magnify the pain. *Whatever we resist, persists.* Use the pain as a stimulus for more rhythm and ease. The first and best pain-management skill is to create more ease. Shift the focus from feelings of pain to your breathing rhythm. As you relax and breathe, the quality of your thoughts and imagery will improve and you can bring to mind some positive power thoughts and even some slow-motion, high-performance imagery. Use pain as a stimulus and a reminder to refocus and go deeper into your breathing.

Building your pain tolerance is a measure of mental toughness. Learn and know that you can handle tension and frustration or difficulty better than anybody else.

Experiment with these techniques, become mentally tougher so that nothing takes you off course, not anxiety, frustration, anger, or pain.

"Golf is a compromise between what your
ego wants you to do, what experience tells
you to do, and what your nerves let you do."
– Bruce Crampton

TRAINING EXERCISES

This chapter has four training assignments:

1. Do one 10-to-15-minute conscious breathing session every day. Breathe easily, and imagine yourself golfing with confidence, touch, and excellent form.

2. Whenever you catch yourself experiencing a negative, anxious, or frustrating thought or tense feeling, release it, breathe in energy, and think smooth.

3. Experiment with the simple process of breathing in on the backswing and out on the downswing. Work with these suggestions and see what feels right and easy.

4. In training, think about your breath as a wheel. Work at turning the wheel and generating power whenever you feel the need to increase your emotional intensity or power.

SECTION THREE
RIGHT FOCUS

"The mind is your greatest weapon. It's the greatest club
in your bag. It's also your Achilles' heel."
— Steve Elkington

"It's all about the mindset going into the week."
— Nelly Korda

We are all performers. As a golfer you will play better by developing *right focus*. By "right focus," I mean generating and consistently tuning in to positive thoughts and high-performance images that will help you to excel.

Lydia Ko put it this way: "When you are not performing to the level you should be, of course there's doubt. I know I've doubted myself at times, but I think my team have really helped me to clear those thoughts out and make sure I'm working on the right things. . . . That's all you can do. I think I'm becoming less result-oriented . . . [I] just do a good job focusing on things in my swing or my putting and the mental side I'm working on. And that's it, and I think that puts a little less pressure on me. I know these aspects of my game that need to improve and I'll keep working at it and see where it goes."[1]

CHAPTER FIVE

Power Thinking

"You don't win tournaments by playing well
and thinking poorly." – Lee Westwood

The goals of this chapter are for you to become more aware of how your thinking can influence your performance and to develop a program of power thinking that will really enhance your game.

Positive power thinking is a key to success. We think all the time. The quality of our thoughts has a direct bearing on how we feel and perform. There are three kinds of power thoughts.

1. Technical thoughts
2. Strategy thoughts
3. Personal thoughts

TECHNICAL THOUGHTS AND YOUR ABCS

Your ABCs are technical thoughts you can bring to mind in practice. They will keep you focused on two or three basics (no more) to simplify your game and help you to perform.

Examples of some of my clients' ABCs include the following:

- align to target
- breathe easy
- good tempo
- hips through
- smooth transfer
- flow through

No busy minds, no overthinking. Remember, you should not have more than two or three technical ABCs.

Dick Zokol, a PGA Tour veteran, has developed an interesting approach to getting golfers to focus less on the end result — the cause of much anxiety and inconsistency — and more on the process of playing. Dick calls the app program MindTRAK Golf. What Dick did is analyze what he believes makes a good golf shot. He came up with two factors:

1. Accurately assessing the circumstances surrounding the shot (e.g., the distance, the lie, the wind and weather, the fairway and green conditions).

2. Then — executing the proper golf swing.

After the shot, he recommends evaluating the shot outcome based on how well the shot was performed with regard to two points: Was the shot correctly assessed? Was the shot properly executed?

Dick attests that by focusing on these two markers and not on the score, you will stay more in the present, play with less stress and anxiety, and ultimately be more successful. He goes on to say that most golf coaches focus on swing fundamentals. He feels his new approach addresses what he calls "mental thought fundamentals," enabling the golfer (and the golfer's coach) to more precisely analyze the golfer's game. The process indicates whether the golfer needs to improve their assessment of the shot or their execution of the swing. Zokol believes this approach focuses the golfer in the present and removes the thought and angst related to the result.[1]

As a sport psychologist working with golfers, I think the approach does provide some clarity of focus and may help some golfers to reduce their score consciousness. Regarding Zokol's first factor, I agree that developing an effective golf routine should include a proper assessment of the circumstances (e.g., distance, weather, course layout and conditions). However, I also believe an important aspect of one's routine should support the golfer feeling balanced and at ease as he or she approaches the shot. Regarding Zokol's second factor, I also agree that executing the swing and not focusing on the score should promote more effective play. However, easier said than done. Again, to be in the *present*, to *feel* the swing, to play with athleticism and instinct, and to *avoid thinking about mechanics, result, and score*, my best advice is to work with conscious breathing and the release reflex outlined in Chapters 3 and 4.

Focus is key, and I concur with David Leadbetter's advice cited earlier, "Your final goal is to convert your athletic swing to pure instinct rather than conscious thought."[2] Or, with Curtis Strange, who said, "Under pressure, one of the most important things I have to remember is to breathe."[3] Or, Tom Watson, who said, "When I learned how to breathe, I learned how to win."[4]

STRATEGY THOUGHTS

These are thoughts we think about prior to playing a course, a hole, or a shot. Essentially, these thoughts provide an image or flexible guideline as to how to play the shot — or the golf course.

PERSONAL THOUGHTS

Your personal thoughts describe the way you think about yourself as a golfer. They reflect self-image and a general sense of confidence. Early in my mental coaching process, I encourage golfers to think of themselves in a positive way.

The "homework" exercise I give them is this: *Every morning* after you wake up, look at yourself in the mirror, make eye contact, and say to yourself, "I am a good golfer" (or, if you feel that you are a work in progress, say to yourself, "I am becoming a good golfer"). Then, list four or five strengths that you have as a golfer. Typical responses include

- "I'm smart. I have a good sense of the sport. I read the course and my abilities well."
- "I have a variety of reliable strokes."
- "I have a smooth, full swing."
- "I strike the ball well."
- "I'm strong, long, and straight off the tee."
- "My short game/chipping is good."
- "I have good touch."
- "I'm a good putter."
- "I'm mentally tough."

Every time you go to work out, to practice, or to play, know that you are a good golfer and remind yourself of your strengths.

Gary Player, one of golf's greats, on the power of positive thought: "As a boy of 15 years old I was consumed by the game. I would stand in front of a mirror and say over and over, 'You're the greatest golfer in the world.' It was absurd but something told me that it mattered."[5]

SELF-RATING SCALE

Self-evaluation can highlight your strengths and weaknesses. Once you are aware of your strengths and weaknesses, work to strengthen your strengths and to improve those areas in which you need improvement. For the greatest benefit, it's important to be completely honest with yourself in doing this assessment. Also, understand this is *a training exercise* and should be done well before and NOT immediately before a competition.

Rate yourself on the following categories on a scale of 1 to 7 (1 being very weak/poor and 7 being very strong/excellent).

Rate Your Golf Smarts

Your ability to read the course and use your strengths to best advantage: _____

Rate Your Motivation

To what degree are you totally committed to being the best golfer you can be: _____

Your commitment to fitness training: _____

Your commitment to skills/swing mechanics training: _____

Your commitment to mental training: _____

Rate Your Fitness

Your overall fitness: _____

Your strength for golf: _____

Your mental fitness: _____

Your fitness compared to other club/team members: _____

Rate Your Skill

With woods: _____

With irons: _____

When chipping: _____

When putting: _____

Rate Your Emotional Management

Your competitive confidence: _____

Your ability to be calm under pressure: _____

How much you love to compete: _____

Your ability to stay positively focused (nothing takes you off track): _____

The idea is to use these ratings as a guide to determine which areas you should maintain and which areas you need to strengthen.

"Doubt yourself and you doubt everything.
Judge yourself and you see judges
everywhere. But if you listen to the sound of
your own voice, you can rise above doubt
and judgment." – Nancy Lopez

POWER WORDS

These words should be so strong that they create a feeling and a picture that increases your power and potential. There are many kinds of power words you can use. Be creative. Be a hunter. Be in the moment.

The use of power words can be extremely helpful in dealing with the intense pressure that is often a part of competition. Here's an example of how I used power words to help a team of cyclists prepare for the Olympics that resulted in their riding an incredible race.

I was asked to work with Canada's Time Trial Team (TTT) in preparation for the Olympic Games. TTT is a four-person bicycle race in which the four riders race in a straight line, changing the lead person every 30 to 40 seconds as they race. The team had to make the specific qualifying time of two hours five minutes and 10 seconds (2:05:10) for the 100 km distance. Prior to that, the Canadian team's record was 2:06:40. In other words, they had to take a minute and 30 seconds off their best time ever just to qualify. After some relaxation and conscious breathing training, I asked the four riders what specific thoughts and feelings come to mind when they are racing that could cause them to tighten up and lose power. They identified three "biggies": *fear, pain*, and *difficulty*.

Fear: The fears include losing control, breaking down, failure, embarrassment, not keeping the pace, crashing, getting injured, and letting the team down. For most of us, fear is a high-frequency performance thought. It's one that can stimulate action or cause tension and contraction, limit breathing, and reduce power.

Pain: The pain most frequently experienced in cycling is so intense that a rider can't physically continue to race. Some even pass out on their bicycles. Then there is the psychic pain that cyclists and all athletes experience in relation to the possibility of a failed performance. Psychic pain threatens the ego. Like physical pain, it can also cause contraction, limit breathing, and cut down power.

Difficulty: Under race circumstances, thoughts and feelings like "this is too hard," "it's impossible," "there's no way," and "I can't do this" also cause contraction, limit breathing, and diminish power.

I asked each TTT rider to come up with a single power thought that they could tune in to whenever they experience fear, pain, or difficulty. The thought was to be a simple and powerful one, a single word that was personally meaningful and that stimulated a positive feeling and gave them energy. It had to be simple and brief because the stress and fatigue of a race can express itself like static, making it difficult to think. I wanted a power word that would be comprehensible and useful under pressure.

Each rider selected a different word. Brian, the team captain, chose the word *more*. Whenever he experienced pain, fatigue, self-doubt, or negativity, he would think "more," turn the wheel, and push a little harder, a little longer, or a little faster.

Yvon chose the word *smooth*. He was a big guy who knew that under pressure he tended to tighten up and that caused him to have to work harder to accomplish the same result.

Chris chose the word *machine*. He wanted to experience himself as inhuman and impervious to pain, doubt, and difficulty. Whenever he noticed himself tuning in to a limiting thought or feeling, Chris would take a breath, draw in energy, turn the wheel, think "machine," and accelerate.

And Dave chose the word *fast*. It sparked in him the image to be lighter, tougher, more aggressive and streamlined. He brought that power word to mind whenever he felt stressed.

Part of their psychological training addressed dealing effectively with the considerable pain, tension, and difficulty produced by that grueling event. I explained to each rider that the natural reaction to fear, pain, and difficulty is to contract, to tighten up, and to try to hold on. I also explained that it is much easier to be aggressive than to hold on. Holding on doesn't change anything. It just means that you attempt to ride the race in the state of being tense and contracted. And it is way more difficult to be fast and to endure in that contracted, limited state. Along with thought management, riders spent considerable time with the conscious breathing and release techniques (described in Chapters 3 and 4), so that if/when they felt fear, pain, or difficulty they could focus on breathing, turning the wheel, and tuning in to their positive power word.

At the start of the race, the team went out very fast. After 20 km, Chris reported that he started to feel pain and began to think, "I hurt. I won't be able to keep this pace." Then, he thought, "Just hold on." When he realized what he was thinking, he reminded himself: *It's easier to be aggressive than to hold on*. He went deeper into his breathing, refocused on the word "machine," and picked up his pace. Again, about 70 km into the race, Chris became focused on and locked into pain. Again, the negative thoughts followed — "I can't continue" — and he caught himself, refocused on his breathing and on being like a "machine." He rode right through the pain. He rode a great race. The whole team did.

What makes this story relevant is the end result. The riders went out at a fast pace and stayed focused and aggressive throughout the race. Dave, Chris, and Yvon all mentioned to me afterwards that at times they were hurting and entertained the thoughts of "I can't do it" and "I can't go on." When they noticed themselves tuning in to those negative thoughts and feelings, they remembered to go deeper into their breathing, to turn the wheel, to generate more power, and to refocus on their power word.

The end result was they rode the 100 km distance in an amazing 1:51:10. Their time was an astonishing 15 minutes and 30 seconds faster than the previous Canadian record and an unofficial world record in that event. What is also remarkable is that it wasn't a new team of superstars imported from another part of the planet or the galaxy. Three of the four racers had been part of the team that set the 2:06:40 TTT record the year before. What was different now was that all the key elements were in place. They were well coached — which is to say, the right people were selected — they knew what to do, and they were in excellent shape. And they were trained to manage their minds aggressively, to change limiting thoughts and feelings, and to stay tuned in to winning programs using their power words.

If you experience any negative, tensing thoughts (fear, difficulty), release them, breathe in, and refocus on a power word. A few power words and thoughts golf clients have suggested are focus, smooth, breathe, "Yes, I can," or as the Nike slogan goes, "Just do it."

AFFIRMATIONS

Johnny Miller is cited as saying, "My dad was always about affirmations, 'You're doing great. . . . You're on the right track. . . . Keep doing those exercises. . . . You're going to be a champion.' Over and over, he'd call me 'champ' . . . that affirmation of potential. Actually, not just potential 'cause I knew when I was 9 years old, I was going to be a champion golfer . . . that affirmation of greatness or being successful from your father is the strongest affirmation there is for a boy."[6]

Here are some thoughts to repeat to yourself. After each thought, take a breath. Remember, thoughts precede action, and repetition builds strength.

- I play smooth.
- I swing free.
- I see it . . . I feel it . . . I do it.
- My breath is a source of calm and power.
- I strike the ball well.
- I hit long and straight.
- My short game is my strength.
- I have good touch on and around the green.

- I make my putts.
- I make good reads.
- I have great touch.
- Soft hands . . . cats' feet . . . clear eyes.
- I'm mentally tough.
- I am committed to be the best I can be.
- My mind is a force I use to make things happen.
- I deserve to express all of my ability.
- I find something positive in every situation.
- I am a winner and I enjoy winning.
- Self-love is allowing myself to be great.
- I can tune out negative and anxious thoughts.
- I breathe in energy and power.
- I love pressure.

Select affirmations: Review the affirmations above. Determine which ones may work for you and select those that relate to your situation, that address your strengths or aspects of golf that you want to develop, or those that just help you to feel good.

Select the six to eight affirmations or power thoughts that would help you to become a more consistent, effective golfer. Write them down and repeat them to yourself often. You can say your affirmations to yourself or write them in the first person (e.g., "I love pressure") or in the second person (e.g., "You love pressure"). The first person is personal and powerful.

Words are like food for the spirit. They can nurture us. Just as you eat food that you like, it's important that you say things to yourself that feel good and that give you power. Repetition of these words and phrases builds strength. Repeat these power words and thoughts to yourself frequently. Develop a positive mental focus and attitude. In relaxing and challenging situations, take a breath and affirm the positive. The positive feeling should come first. It helps you to believe in the things you are repeating. If you match the positive feeling with the positive thought, you create a loop that feeds itself with positive energy.

"As an athlete, as a competitor, you have to believe in yourself." – Tiger Woods

"Achievement is largely the product of steadily raising one's level of aspiration and expectation." – Jack Nicklaus

TRAINING EXERCISES

1. Every morning (during your golf season), shortly after waking up, look in the mirror, make eye contact, and remind yourself that you are a good golfer, and tell yourself four or five reasons why. Every time you go to practice or compete, know you are a good golfer. Know your strengths.

2. Complete the self-evaluation scale above and select and record three or four strengths you are going to focus on making even stronger, and one or two weaknesses you are going to work to eliminate. There is some evidence to suggest that working on as many or more weaknesses than strengths is discouraging and undermines perseverance and confidence.

3. Select six to eight affirmations. Repeat them daily — in the morning and/or before training and during training. Some people record their affirmations; others write them out and tape a list of their favorites to the mirror and look at themselves while repeating them.

CHAPTER SIX

High-Performance Imagery

"Visualization is the most powerful thing we have."
— Nick Faldo

"I practice visualization. The clearer you can visualize the
shot the greater chance the body has of reproducing it. If
you don't have a clear picture before you hit, the shot will
come up fuzzy." — Brad Bryant

The goal of this chapter is to explore different ways you can use imagery
to enhance your performance and well-being. Images are fundamental.
We experience images even before we use words. Imagery is a powerful performance aid for athletes and an essential aspect of being able
to focus.

We will examine three basic kinds of imagery:

1. Goal imagery (imagining the end result)
2. Stimulating imagery
3. Mental rehearsal

GOAL IMAGERY – IMAGINING A SUCCESSFUL END RESULT

Create and hold the image of exactly what it is that you are working toward. That can be both your ultimate goal in golf (e.g., NCAA scholarship, club championship, knocking 10 strokes off your game) or it can be the end result of an upcoming competition or match. As stated in Chapter 1, a clear, meaningful goal is a driver. It pushes you to do the physical, technical, and mental preparation to make that result a reality.

Most sport psychologists would agree that it is more important to focus on the process of getting there than to think of the end result. However, seeing is believing, and clarifying intention with an end-result image can mobilize a process that puts powerful unconscious forces to work for you. It can also sustain you and help you to endure the training and inevitable challenges necessary to get you where you want to go.

Albert Einstein summed up the importance of imagery in leading to successful end results when he said, "Imagination is everything. It is the preview of life's coming attractions."[1]

In keeping with Einstein's comment, Eric Wang, a CPGA golf coach, related two anecdotes from his time as a golfer on the University of California Irvine golf team. He recalled that in his sophomore year, a sport psychologist spoke to the team. One of the things he asked the golfers to imagine was what they would do differently if they knew that in five years, they would be a PGA Tour winner. Eric said almost all the golfers said they would behave differently. Their responses included seeing themselves differently, carrying themselves differently, practicing differently, and feeling less pressured and less uptight. According to Eric, the positive effects of this winning image unfortunately didn't last very long.

Then, in his senior year, Eric was a key part of the UC Irvine golf team that went to the NCAA Division 1 golf championships, which were held that year at Duke University. Duke had just won the national

NCAA basketball championship and at a banquet in the Duke gymnasium, Mike Krzyzewski, Duke's legendary basketball coach, addressed all the collegiate golfers. Years later, Eric recalled what impressed him again was the power of positive visualization. Coach K told these young, talented golfers that every day before the big March Madness basketball tournament, he had his players relax and visualize themselves as winners — having just won the national championship, feeling that feeling, and seeing themselves holding up the trophy.[2]

As we did in Chapter 1, imagine your ultimate golf goal. See it. Create a mental picture of you having achieved success, feeling proud, and with a big smile on your face. Now think about and make a list of the effort and training you are going to have to do to make that goal a reality.

Take dead aim. Another expression of goal imagery is to visualize the end result of the shot you are about to take. Before every shot, take aim and visualize the shot you want to make. Visualize it in HD. See the target. See the trajectory of the ball going to the target. See the ball going where you want it to go. Make it part of your shot routine.

Harvey Penick, Master golf coach and author of *Harvey Penick's Little Red Book*, wrote, "I can't say it too many times. Take dead aim. It is the most important advice in this book. Make it a point to do it every time on every shot. Don't just do it from time to time when you happen to remember. Take dead aim."[3]

On taking dead aim, Tiger Woods described how he plays shots: "I putt to the picture. I take into account all the information, then I am putting to the picture . . . or hitting my golf shot to my picture. That gets rid of all the mechanical thoughts."[4]

STIMULATING IMAGERY

Stimulating images are images that many athletes use to create a positive, powerful, competitive focus and feeling.

As humans there is an aspect of our being that is almost angelic. It is that remarkable capacity we have to envision things . . . and manifest them. We set a goal, we imagine it, we work/train to make it happen, and then it does.

In addition to that visioning aspect of our being, there is an animal component as well. We *are* animals after all, not plants. I regularly ask athletes, "Pick an animal, one that would give you the qualities you want to have when you're performing at your best." Of the elite athletes I ask, 99 percent choose predators.

In golf, along with Eldrick "Tiger" Woods, a few other notable predator nicknames are Jack Nicklaus (Golden Bear), Greg Norman (Great White Shark), Corey Pavin (Bulldog), Dustin Johnson (Cheetah), and Ben Hogan (the Hawk).

Question: What is the difference between the golfer who is the predator and the one who is the prey?

The predator golfer is positive and assertive. The predator golfer steps onto the tee, fairway, or green with the thought and feeling of making a fine shot. The prey golfer is anxious. He or she worries about negative possibilities and their thinking is often "Don't miss" or "Don't make a mistake."

The animals that most golfers select are the big cats: tigers, lions, cheetahs, leopards, jaguars, panthers. Some have picked predatory birds like eagles and hawks; others have picked foxes, wolves, and sharks. These animals are hunters. They have focus and power. The power animal you choose should stimulate and represent you at your best. This is you physically strong, well coordinated, with balance, precision, and power . . . not overthinking but rather trusting your instincts. One other quality about these predators is that they don't care what others think — they just hunt.

Dustin Johnson framed this nicely after winning the 2020 Masters when he said, "I kind of looked at the leaderboard a little bit early and then after that I just told myself, 'Don't worry about what anybody's doing, just play as good as you can.'"[5]

If the prey should elude a predator, the predator has no negative self-judgment; it simply goes after another prey. In golf, it's always *next shot*. Again, there's no negative self-judgment. After a good shot or a poor shot, you simply take a breath and move on to hunting/playing the next shot well. Nancy Lopez in Chapter 4 states this well: "When you have a bad shot, you have to shake it off, take a breath, and bring an excited attitude to the next shot. If you keep the bad shot feeling, you are more likely to hit the next one poorly too. I always stepped up to the next shot with the attitude that I am going to make my best swing and hit this one great!"[6]

Exercise: Select the image of an animal that appeals to you. Think about breathing in energy and firing up the tiger, panther, cheetah, eagle, or wolf. Be a hunter — powerful, focused, and sharp.

Mike was a sensitive young professional golfer struggling to stay afloat on one of the lesser tours. When I asked him how the work we were about to do might be helpful, he replied that he wasn't feeling comfortable or confident and (not surprisingly) wasn't performing close to his potential. He said he played as if he didn't really believe in himself. In some tournaments when he was playing well, he wouldn't finish strong.

As we worked through the program, I asked Mike to choose an animal that would give him the qualities he would like to have if he were playing his best golf. After some reflection, Mike said, "an old dog." When I asked him what kind of old dog, Mike replied, "a golden retriever." While almost all elite athletes select predators (tigers, lions, wolves, bears, eagles, sharks — all assertive hunters), the retriever is best known as a friendly companion dog. I explained to Mike that while his choice was a comforting one, it didn't really embody qualities that would support him asserting himself and closing under pressure. And then I asked Mike to reconsider. He did and after some thought selected a lion. When I asked him why he chose the lion, he said it was because a lion is confident, proud — the king — and an effective predator that could finish. When we spoke a few days later, Mike reported that the lion image gave him a different, more confident feeling on the golf course.

MENTAL REHEARSAL

Mental rehearsal means actually practicing in your mind the things you want to do on the course. Remember, you get more of what you think about. One of my favorite exercises to improve mental rehearsal is to ask a golfer to complete the following sentence: "When I'm playing golf at my best, I _____."

Fill in the blank with five to six action images of what you would see if you were golfing great. These super action images should give you a clear sense of what it would *look* and *feel* like when you are performing well.

We know that deliberate practice on swing mechanics and creating the golf feel you want to have lead to improvement. This is true in physical practice. It's also true using visualization, especially in that relaxed alpha brain wave state.

> "Mental rehearsal is just as important as
> physical rehearsal." – Phil Mickelson

One of the most remarkable examples of mental rehearsal and the power of visualization is the experience of George Robert Hall. Colonel George Hall was a USAF fighter pilot who was shot down over North Vietnam on September 27, 1965. Colonel Hall spent the next seven years in horrendous conditions as a POW in Hoa Lo Prison in Hanoi. For much of that time, he was held in isolation and tortured. He subsisted on a meager diet of approximately 300 calories per day. During his con-finement, Hall used his love of golf and his visualization skills not only to help sustain him but remarkably also to maintain his golf game. He described how *every day* he would visualize putting on his golf apparel, heading to the golf course, and playing each hole on his home course. He would imagine the sights and sounds of the course, the fairways, greens, trees, and roughs. He would imagine himself standing behind the hole, aligning the shot, then going through his setup. He described placing his left hand over the thumb of his right hand to create the sen-sation of gripping the club, setting his wrists, taking the club back to the top of the swing, and then bringing the club down while focusing on the part of the ball he wanted to hit . . . and even hearing the sound of the club face striking the ball. And after making his final putt, Colonel Hall would imagine writing down the score for each hole.[7]

What makes this story even more remarkable is that after his release from seven and a half years of captivity, on February 12, 1973, less than six weeks later, George Hall was invited to play golf in the Greater New Orleans POW Pro-Am Open, where he shot a 76. This was after seven years of deprivation, after having lost almost 100 pounds, and after not picking up a golf club or having any physical conditioning. What George Hall did have was a great spirit, a strong will, a love of golf, and the power of visualization.

Before selecting a club and stepping up to the ball, Jack Nicklaus used mental rehearsal and visualized the shot and the swing. Jack said, "I never hit a shot, even in practice, without having a very sharp, in-focus picture of it in my head. It's like a color movie. First, I 'see' the ball where I want it to finish, nice and white and sitting up high on the bright green grass. Then the scene quickly changes, and I 'see' the ball going there: its path, trajectory, and shape, even its behavior on landing. Then there's sort of a fade-out, and the next scene shows me making the kind of swing that will turn the previous images into reality."[8]

Master golf coach Jim Flick, who coached Nicklaus, has said, "Throughout his career Jack was very good at practicing mechanics but playing by feel. A mechanical thought is something like, 'Increase your hip turn.' Poor players use mechanical thoughts on the range then use those same thoughts on the course. That doesn't allow the body to react to playing conditions or the swing to flow."[9]

The message is clear: Think about it; see the shot you want to make and the swing that will make it happen. Then take a breath and switch out of thought and imagine/feel your smooth, natural swing . . . then feel you striking the ball well.

Golf Routines: A golf routine can be very helpful. Routines provide consistency. You are the boss. Create a golf routine you are comfortable with: a routine that gives you the feeling and focus you desire and one that you don't have to think about. Davis Love Jr. has said, "A routine is not a routine if you've got to think about it."[10]

Imagery can be a key part of a positive performance routine. Use it before setting up for every shot whether you are on the tee, walking down the fairway, or about to putt on the green:

- Experience the moment.
- Feel where you are by taking a couple of calming, empowering breaths.
- Visualize the shot you want to make. Site your target and take dead aim. Visualize the ball going to the target.
- Take a couple of practice swings to re-create the feeling you had when you made that shot.
- Step up to the ball, site the target, release any tension, and breathe . . .
- Let your feelings flow as you strike the ball to the target.

More on routines from CPGA Golf Coach Eric Wang: "Assess the lie of the ball, whether it's a clean lie in the middle of the fairway, sitting up in the rough, or sitting down buried in thick rough, decide on your game plan and how you will execute the shot. Picture the trajectory and the landing spot, or target, and how the ball will react when it lands."

Explore using imagery to improve your chipping and putting.

CHIPPING

Here's what Coach Wang had to say on this subject: "Often when golfers approach chip shots, they put a lot of pressure on themselves, whether needing to get it up and down (one chip/one putt), or telling themselves not to duff it, shank it, chunk it, etc. These negative thoughts, known as the chipping yips, can create doubt and tension. To combat this, one strategy I employ to show students how to approach a chip shot, is to change what they focus on. Before setting up for the chip shot I would first walk them over to the hole and we will survey the break around the hole. Then we will walk back to the ball and pick a flat landing spot where we want the ball to land. By choosing a flat landing spot, you can better predict how the golf ball will react when it lands and rolls out like a putt. Then we assess the lie and select the club needed to execute the right trajectory to pull off the shot. This process of working backwards from the hole to the landing spot to the ball allows us to get our creative (right) side of the brain working rather than the brain focusing on mechanical thoughts. We now start to play with our eyes and focus more on what we want the ball to do rather than worrying about trusting our swings. This technique has helped many golfers to stay in the moment when chipping.

"Once you have your game plan for the shot, do a few practice swings behind the ball to rehearse the feel. Then address the ball and commit to the target. Once you're standing over the ball, it is important that there are NO swing thoughts or swing mechanics going through your mind, rather only the swing feelings you've just rehearsed and the target you're aiming at."[11]

PUTTING

In his *Little Red Book*, Harvey Penick outlined his "simple system for putting":

1. Read your line to the hole from behind the ball.

2. Approach the ball from behind and take your stance with hands slightly ahead of the ball.

3. Glance at the hole and then glance at your putter blade to make sure it is square to your line.

4. Take one, two, or three practice strokes, judging the distance and concentrating on each one as if you are trying to make the putt.

5. Put your putter blade down behind the ball, keep your head and eyes still, and imitate your last practice stroke.

Penick believed that one great value of this system was that it puts your mind on the stroke and not on the importance of the putt. And on this subject Harvey Penick was emphatic: "Never — I repeat never — allow yourself to think what is riding on the putt, whether it's a major championship or a 50-cent wager." Instead, he advised concentrating on imitating your practice stroke, *not* on what will happen if either you miss or make it.[12]

Ben Crenshaw, an exceptional putter, agrees, saying, "When I putted the best, I had a blank mind. I wasn't really thinking about anything. Nothing but the path and how hard to hit it."[13]

Following a round at the Sanderson Farms Championship, Sergio Garcia was asked why he closed his eyes after addressing the ball and before taking the club back on his putting stroke. He said he had been doing it for a while because focusing on the ball throughout led to his trying to be too perfect, whereas closing his eyes briefly relaxes him and helps him feel and trust his natural stroke better.[14] (Interesting: Closing the eyes and taking a breath is an effective way to reduce anxiety by switching from beta brain waves to alpha brain waves. Try it before putting.)

Let's just summarize what the experts are saying: Whether you are playing off the fairway, chipping, or putting, they all agree you'll play more effectively if you are calm, have a clear target image, release thoughts about swing mechanics or the consequence of the shot, and feel the stroke. Easier said than done.

Coach Eric says that it's important there are no swing thoughts or swing mechanics going through your mind when you are standing over the ball, only the swing feelings you just rehearsed and the target you're aiming at. Coach Harvey advises you to put your mind on the stroke and not on the importance or what is riding on the putt. Ben Crenshaw said, "When I putted best, I had a blank mind."

Okay, so how can you do those things? Understand people tend to do under pressure what they have previously done under pressure. Golfers who tend to think mechanics and outcome and tighten up before a pressure shot will probably do the same before the next pressure shot *unless they over-train themselves with conscious breathing and release-reflex techniques in a relaxed setting.* In so doing, they develop the habit to be calmer and more feeling and trusting of their stroke. So, again, I recommend you work with the training exercises in Chapters 3 and 4 and become an expert in emotional management.

In addition, one's attitude to a precision-demanding situation like putting is also important. Negative thoughts and feelings create stress and reduce performance. Positive thoughts and feelings enhance performance. Ben Crenshaw is also alleged to have said that he loved every putting green he'd played on.

Now let's assume that you want to do some mental rehearsal for a challenging upcoming competition. Create a mental picture of the course and competition. Imagine a good start to the match . . . you feel confident, swing well . . . you are a tiger or an eagle hunting . . . strong and patient, calm and composed. Before and after each shot, you breathe and refocus . . . nothing takes you off track . . . you are dialed in . . . confident and scoring.

Repetition builds strength. Mental rehearsal is as important as physical practice. Frequent practice with mental rehearsal will help you to develop your mental skill. To improve your golf performance, it's important to imagine and mentally rehearse executing your golf skills properly and effectively.

MAKING YOUR IMAGERY WORK FOR YOU

Imagery is like a motion picture, and you are the director of that mental movie. There's a considerable body of evidence to show that mental rehearsal/watching your own high-performance "movies" will help you to excel. Here are five tips that will enhance your mental rehearsal and help you to direct a high-quality experience:

Clearly define what you want. Uncertainty leads to confusion and stress. As we mentioned, to increase success and reduce stress, create clear HD action images of what you want to do. Using self-talk, remind yourself that you are a good golfer and that you have the ability to really excel. See and feel yourself as a successful and confident golfer, performing well. Greg Norman's comment that "Happiness is a long walk with a putter,"[15] evokes a positive image and a good feeling.

Relax, then imagine. Whenever possible, relax and breathe before putting your creative imagination to work for you. As you do, you increase the flow of alpha brain waves and the quality of your images will become stronger, clearer, and more positive. Just taking a moment or two to breathe will make it easier for you to imagine yourself performing at your best. In golf that may mean being focused, smooth, sharp, confident, and composed.

Stay positive. You will get more of what you imagine. Stay focused on the image of you at your best. If you are about to play a round of golf, begin your mental rehearsal imagining yourself going through your shot routine, then visualize a great shot on the first hole. Visualize as many quality shots as you can. The only value of running a negative thought of something that didn't work is to determine what you can do to change it and enhance your golf performance.

Be dynamic and brief. Create imagery that is a short, dynamic movie clip, not a snapshot. Most golfers find their imagery is most effective if they imagine themselves from the perspective of playing on the course. Others visualize their performance as if they were a spectator in the stands watching themselves perform. It has been suggested that imagining oneself as the player is preferable before and during a match, and visualizing oneself as an observer is preferable after a match. Try both approaches and see what works best for you.

Use all your senses. Make your mental rehearsal multisensory. Most people are strongly visual and many think imagery is simply visual. Golf has very strong tactile and kinesthetic elements. Incorporate all the sensory cues into your mental rehearsal. See it, feel it, hear it — and when appropriate, you can even smell it.

TRAINING EXERCISES

Practice is essential to incorporate the imagery suggestions offered in this chapter.

1. Continue to work with affirmations. Select eight to 10 favorite power thoughts. Continue to repeat them several times a day, as you did previously.

2. Select the image of a successful goal or end result — something that you want to experience or achieve. It's important to have a picture of what you're striving for. Put that image in your mind — clarifying intention is

empowering. Reflecting on that image can give you the energy to carry on and to realize your goals. Every once in a while, sit back and imagine having achieved that goal. It's been said that what the mind can conceive and believe, it can achieve. Feel it, see it, believe it, and do it.

3. Think of an animal that gives you the qualities you would like to have when you're playing your best golf: vision, focus, power, determination. Select an animal that can stimulate your game and give you a hunter's focus. Work hard and enjoy the challenge.

4. Select six high-performance action images that you would see if you were golfing at your best. These are images that evoke a feeling — visualize them, feel them. These high-performance action images can help you sharpen the edge and prepare to compete.

CHAPTER SEVEN

Exceptional Performances –
The Sub-60 Club

At present, only two golfers have recorded rounds of 55 on regulation golf courses. As they reflect on their remarkable performances, see what you can you take from their experience that might help you with your game.

On May 12, 2012, Rhein Gibson, a PGA Tour player shot a remarkable 55 (12 birdies and two eagles) at the River Oaks Golf Club, in Edmond, Oklahoma. Here's some of what Rhein had to say when we spoke about the mental game and that super round of golf.[1]

> SAUL: Rhein, when you reflect back on that day when you shot 55, can you recall anything special about how you focused, or what you felt, or how you were thinking?
>
> RHEIN: Yeah, I was pretty calm, but intense inside. I felt invincible, almost like I knew when I was standing over some of the putts, I just knew that it was going to go in the hole. It was a momentous round. I made a birdie, I made an eagle, I made a birdie and another birdie. My performance was always there. I felt that once I got to that peak-performance point my intensity kind of leveled

off . . . and it didn't go down. I kept it up there the whole way through.

There was a period in my round right where we made the turn. I had just shot 10 under on the back nine and we went to the first hole, and the first hole on this course was kind of difficult and we had to wait 10 or 15 minutes for the two-tee start. The last thing I wanted to do was to think about the toughest tee shot on the course and think about how it could mess up my 10 under on the back nine. So I just kind of talked with my friends about what was coming up for us. And once I got up on the tee box, I was ready to go. And I made a good shot down the fairway. Obviously, golf is a sport where you don't want to be too focused on, and thinking too much about, the end result . . . because the only thing you can affect is what is right in front of you, this shot. Whether it's a tee shot, a fairway shot, or something on the green, your focus should just be on that shot. And then, when you add it all up at the end, well, then that's your end result. And that day it happened to be 55.

SAUL: What happens if some days you don't like how you are feeling. Is there something you can do to change the feeling?

RHEIN: Well, something I learned a number of years ago — a guy taught me some sport psychology stuff. One thing he recommended was that I give my subconscious a name. And when I'm not feeling positive, when I don't feel that great, he said talk to my subconscious, highlight it, and say like, "You get out of my head. This is what I'm going to do. I'm not going to do what you are subconsciously telling me to do." And whenever I feel in those situations, especially on a day when it's not going great, I tell myself that. Then I just focus a hundred percent on what I can control, whether it's putting the ball in the hole or on the fairway. And whether it happens or not, just be happy that I actually highlighted it and am still one hundred percent committed. Because in the end, that's all I can do.

SAUL: Tim Gallwey, the author of *The Inner Game of Tennis* and *The Inner Game of Golf*, wrote that there are two minds, Mind 1 and Mind 2. Mind 2 basically knows how to perform. It knows how to swing the club or the racket to hit the ball. Mind 1 is like a critic — watching, judging, criticizing, applying pressure, and saying things like, "Don't do this," "Not too fast." Sometimes [though Gallwey doesn't say this] you have to say to Mind 1, "Shut up."[2]

RHEIN: Yup, exactly.

SAUL: I work a lot with breathing because if you are focused on your breathing, you stay in the present. You are into this breath, and then it's this breath. It keeps you in the now.

RHEIN: I can see that. And I'd add to that, when I am playing my best, I'm not adjusting my swing. My movements are the same. I'm not quicker or I'm not slower. And I like to sing. I don't know if it's a relaxing thing. It has my brain focused on the one thing rather than on my subconscious, which incidentally, I named "the weasel," and I tell the weasel to get the f—— out of my head. That's the way I look at it.

SAUL: Well, I think singing is brilliant . . . because it's a breathing thing and it's a flow thing, there's rhythm and tempo, and it's a happy thing.

RHEIN: In fact, the morning I shot that round, one of the last songs I listened to on my way to the course was the song I sang all day.

SAUL: Which song was what? Do you remember what it was?

RHEIN: Yeah, it was a country band called the Eli Young Band and the song was . . . I have to look back on it . . . something like, "Even if it breaks your heart." It was a good country song. You know country music is not upbeat — it's not down beat — it's like a constant and it's just something that kind of kept me the same rather than up and down.

SAUL: Well, I think singing is a good technique, and it just makes sense. As I said, I work with breathing, which may not be as much fun as singing . . .

RHEIN: For me, if I'm singing, all I'm thinking about is the song. There's no room for that subconscious in my brain.

SAUL: So, recalling that day, do you think you were singing between shots as you played the round?

RHEIN: Very much so.

SAUL: Identity is another important thing I talk about in this book [Chapter 10]. Psychologists know that if somebody performs very well, say on an IQ test, it tells us they are intelligent, that they have ability. However, if they perform poorly, it doesn't necessarily mean a lack of ability. They could have been hammered the night before. Maybe they were indifferent, they didn't care, or they simply weren't motivated to perform and weren't paying attention. But a good score always tells us about ability. And I believe it's the same in golf. If a golfer named Rhein goes out and shoots a round with 12 birdies and two eagles, it certainly says something very positive about his ability and who he is. And I think that individual should feed himself some of that positive kind of self-talk, like, "That's who I am." Because the flip side also happens. When someone who doesn't feel very good about their game is having a really good round and it comes down to the final two or three holes and somewhere in their subconscious "the weasel" is thinking, "This isn't me. I'm not that good," often enough they blow up.

RHEIN: Absolutely. My whole thought was, once I got to 13 under and I had four holes left, to keep my focus. My goal that day was to shoot in the 50s. I had never done that before, but once I had passed that threshold, instead of thinking, "Let's get this to the house," I was thinking, "Let's birdie every hole coming in." That was my mentality. I wanted to stay positive and keep birdie-ing holes instead of being on cruise control and just kind of band-aiding it to the clubhouse. I wasn't happy with 13 under. I thought, "I know I'm playing well. I'm putting good. Let's give myself four more chances coming in and let's see how silly this can be."

I kind of had a bad break on that next hole. I had a chunk of mud on my ball and the ball went straight right, kind of toward the out-of-bounds. Luckily, we got up there and it was just in. And it was a par 5 hole, and that was my second shot. So, on the third shot, I was trying to get it just on the green and see if I could make the putt. I had a difficult shot and I made a par. It kind of pissed me off 'cause I knew it was an easy birdie hole. But it also lit a fire in me and refocused me to say, "Let's just birdie the last three holes," and be thinking, "Let's give myself the best opportunities" and "Where do I need to be on the green to have the easiest putt?" That was my thinking. And I birdied 7, 8, and 9 to finish.

SAUL: That's interesting, because the way you describe it, there's certainly an element of intensity to your game . . . but it also sounds like it was fun.

RHEIN: It was fun. Yeah. I think that hole and that kind of bad break just flicked that level of intensity again and woke me up a little bit to say, "That's okay, you still have three holes to do it," rather than go the other way and get pissed off and maybe try to play too aggressive, and then make a mistake coming in.

SAUL: Well, I believe the two core human emotions are love and fear. Fear is reflected in anxiety, doubt, and uncertainty, and that causes tension and tightness. The other is love, like, "I love the challenge." With love, we embrace the challenge, we step into it and think, "Bring it on." With fear, we tighten up and think, "Don't miss." And while it's easy for me to say this, if a golfer can bring an "I love the challenge" mindset to their game, they play well.

I often use the example of the golfer who makes the great shot and the ball ends up in a bad lie. At that point, the golfer can think, "What the ___ am I supposed to do with this now?" or he can say to himself, "Hey, here's a chance to make a great shot from a bad lie." It's just mindset really.

RHEIN: Absolutely, my first year on Tour when we had all the crowds and stuff around, and I missed a green and if it was a difficult shot or I had a bad lie, like you said, instead of thinking, "Aw . . . that was crap," I'm looking around and thinking, "There's all these people around, let's show off. I'm going to hit this shot within a foot of the hole and listen to the crowd applaud or whatever." So when I had a difficult shot and I was walking up to it, my focus was, "You know what, I'm going to hit the best shot and this crowd is going to love it." I was basically flicking the switch from the negative to that "love feeling" that you are describing.

SAUL: It sounds like you were having a good time . . . and I don't mean that lightly. I mean like, "I'm enjoying this." And how has that changed lately?

RHEIN: I would say, I haven't really been in that same space. For one thing, I haven't got to play much because of Covid. So, it's been like, when I do get to play, I feel like I really have to play well because I just don't have that many opportunities. I'd say I've probably been more on the negative side because at the moment I am too result-oriented. Because I believe I kind of need to. And, on the flip side of that, I need to tell myself, "I play better with this [positive] mental picture." It's a tough balance to find . . . to know that I have to play well . . . and just to free it up so I can enjoy it. So, that's kind of the space I'm in right now.

SAUL: It's interesting. I work with a lot of different sports, maybe 40 different sports over the years. At one time I was the sport psychologist with the NY Mets baseball team. One of the players I was working with was Ray Knight, who was a very good player [and at the time, married to LPGA great Nancy Lopez]. It was the sixth game of the World Series. The Mets were losing the series, 3 games to 2, and losing game six, 5–3 [The game went to extra innings.] There were two out in the bottom of the 10th inning when Ray stepped up to the plate for his turn at bat. Now, what all this meant was that if Ray made an out, his team, the NY Mets, would lose the World Series. It was a real pressure situation. There were 60,000 people in the stands watching and 60 million more watching on television. And all season long, I had been working with Ray, to manage his emotions [with breathing and positive self-talk] and to be able to change thoughts like, "I've got to get a hit," which is tension, to "I love to hit the ball."

It's been said that the only two things you need to do to play well are: 1. assess the shot correctly, and then 2. execute it. And I think that makes sense *except* you have to be able to manage your feelings, especially those intense emotions, to be able to execute your shots effectively and consistently.

And so back to the World Series, Ray knows he doesn't want to feel tight and be thinking, "I've got to get a hit." But there's all this pressure . . . the game is hanging in the balance . . . there's thousands of fans watching in the stadium and millions more watching on TV. Watching the video of that moment, one can see that Ray is trying to use his breathing to get a good feeling going and I'm sure he wants to be thinking, "I love to hit the ball." Of course, he got a hit and his team went on to win the game and the Series, or I wouldn't be using this example.

I think a key element to performing consistently well is to be able to create the feeling to go with the focus. Sometimes people just are in that good space . . . it just happens to be how they are feeling in the moment. But then sometimes that good feeling isn't there and one needs to do something to make that happen. And, Rhein, if anyone could do what you did — the identity-forming part of creating the good feeling is taking a breath and saying to yourself and knowing, "That's who I am." And then it's seeing the shot, loving the challenge, and creating that feeling-state to enable you to execute well.

RHEIN: I agree. I agree. I have to get back to that feeling where I play my best golf, where I'm at 6.5–7 on the graph you showed me earlier (see Chapter 3, figure 3.1). It's been good. I've been working on my game hard. I always think how comfortable you feel about your game is a representation of your attitude and your psyche. I'm excited about what's coming up. I like what you said about "Love the challenge." It's going to be a new slogan for me, for sure.

SAUL: Rhein, it's both about loving the challenge . . . and loving yourself. When I work with breathing, one of the things I tell my clients is that "Self-love allows you to be at your best. And the easiest way to love yourself is to take a breath." Maybe breathing is not 10 out of 10, but it produces something reliable and basic to creating that good feeling. And then again, it's important to be saying positive things to yourself.

On August 27, 2020, Alexander Hughes shot a 55 (10 birdies, two eagles, and one ace) at the South Lakes Golf Course in Tulsa, Oklahoma. Here's our conversation about his remarkable round.[3]

ALEXANDER: It's one of those strange things. I'm sure you've talked to a lot of professional athletes about "the zone." It's almost an out-of-body experience. Everything you're doing is so unrehearsed, and it's just natural. You're just kind of feeling it out, and it feels like the stars are all aligning for you. I knew what I was doing was special. I was in the moment and in the perfect situation. And I just let myself be there on that day. I had no expectations.

I didn't even expect to play that day. I had just regripped my putter three hours before playing that round. I had a new putter grip put on, an old leather Ping putter grip. I wanted something new because I hadn't been putting well lately. I put it on and was letting it dry in my car as I went to the South Links Golf Club. Again, I'm not expecting to play. I'm going out there to see Grant Gudgel, a 14-year-old high school freshman. He had an upcoming tournament there, and a family friend asked me to show him the course. So, I was expecting to let my putter dry in the car and thinking, I'll just walk the course with the kid, take some shots, do some chips, and give him the rundown on the course.

So I meet him on the range. We talk for a bit and he asks me, "Do you want to play?" And I say, "Yeah, sure." I thought, My putter is probably dry; I'll just check it out. And I go to the car and my putter is dry. It felt really good in my hands and I want to go out and play.

Everything started on the second hole. I missed a 10-foot birdie putt on #1. On #2, I hit a perfect high draw from 155 yards and it hit six feet behind the hole and came back right into the cup (for a hole in one). It was a very strange start to the day. I just felt comfortable with Grant. He's really a nice kid. I was playing with no expectations. I parred #3, and then had a string of birdies, #4 through #8.

SAUL: Your lack of expectation and feeling at ease is huge. It's what helps people slip into the zone. On his 55 round, Rhein Gibson mentioned he'd been listening to a country western song on his drive to the golf course, and that song ran though his mind the entire round and kept him loose. He got off to a good start and just worked at staying there.

I don't think there is anybody in the sub-60 club who went out with the thought of breaking 60. Alexander, I think you going out there with no expectation, playing with the kid, feeling loose, getting off to a good start . . . enabled you to express your ability.

ALEXANDER: Exactly. I consider myself a happy person and I always play well when I'm feeling it. I'm a feel player. I feel shots out. I let it come to me. I didn't try to force things, and that was kind of a big thing that happened that day. There was no pressure. I enjoyed being around Grant and helping him out. In between my shots, I was telling him what I think he should be doing for his tournament, which was coming up that weekend. "This is where you need to be on this hole, and on this hole, and this hole." And, after a string of birdies it got crazy when I eagled #9 . . . to shoot 26 on the front. Grant was keeping score and he asked, "Do you know what you just shot?" And I said, "I think I shot 26, or something like that." And he showed me the scorecard and he's shaking his head and he said, "This is the greatest day of my life."

Grant's a freshman at Stillwater High School and he just competed in a six-day state championship, played well, and was top ten as a freshman. He was just an awesome kid to be around and I think it helped.

I don't know what it was. You mentioned Rhein Gibson had the song going through his mind and that may have helped him to stay loose. There wasn't a song. A funny thing was a message I got from Janice Gibson. She is my mentor. She's the director of The First Tee program in Tulsa, and one of the most famous golf people in Oklahoma for how much she's done for the community, helping every person that she can to be a better golfer and ultimately a better person. She's the biggest thing in my life next to my inner family, and I thought of this later on. Janice had played in the US Open back in 2007. She was the last alternate and got the call early Thursday morning to tell her that she was in the tournament. At the time I was 12 years old. When I heard she got in and was going to play, I sent her this long voice mail and I told her to "get her game face on." That's always been our thing. She saved that voice mail . . . and my mom sent it to me a few days ago. I hadn't listened to it, and I happened to listen to it that morning, before playing that round, and maybe it put me in a good mood . . . but I didn't think of it until after.

I didn't think of anything leading up to playing. Then after I thought, "Holy cow! I'm not really sure what just happened." I couldn't do anything wrong. I pushed a couple of putts, and I pulled a couple of putts, and everything wound up dead center in the cup.

SAUL: Nobody is going to shoot a score like that, if their short game doesn't have eyes. You shot 26 on the front.

Starting the back nine seems to be a moment of reflection for the sub-60 club. You mentioned, Grant asked, "Do you know what your score is?" At that point, did you think anything like, "I've got to keep this going. Wow, this is great"? Or any thoughts like, "Don't mess this up"?

ALEXANDER: There wasn't any doubt because I was swinging it well, and whenever you know where the ball is going it's really easy to play well. You just know what you're doing. You know how to set up to hit a certain shot. I didn't really have any doubts. I just told myself, "Just keep swinging the same way."

I never shot in the 50s before. My previous low was a 61, and the back nine is the easier part of this course. So, I just thought, "There's nothing you need to do that's any different than what you've been doing. Just keep doing the same thing, take your time, and be patient." The one thing that could have killed me that day was getting ahead of myself and trying to rush myself. I just tried to stay pretty levelheaded.

Sure enough, I birdied #10, a 360-yard par 4. I'm a longer hitter — that's kind of the difference maker in my game — and I put it green high so it was just a chip, and I get down from there and made another birdie. Eleven was the hole that could have changed the momentum of the round. Instead of hitting a driver, which I would normally have done every time, I pulled out a 3 iron and double-crossed it left. There's an out-of-bounds left on 11. I was probably a yard or two right of the fence. And suddenly I've got a million things going through my mind, like "You just messed it up — why did you do that? You can literally go anywhere to the right, why go left?" So, I get up there and I'm a couple of feet away from the

fence. And, as a right-handed swinger, I know I have
to flip it and go lefty there. So I flipped it over with a
pitching wedge. I've hit the shot before and I know I can
advance it about 60 yards back on the fairway. So I said,
"Take your time. Relax. Make sure you hit the ball solid."
I flipped over my wedge and hit it well, and it goes about
60 yards and I leave myself 96, 97 yards to the pin. And
I put it on the green long right. It's barely on the green,
and I have a 20-foot downhill putt, left to right. I hit a
pretty good putt. I thought I left it about two feet short,
but the greens were rolling really well and it just rolled
out and went in the cup. I just don't know how that went
in. That was a kind of turning point and I said, "OK, I'm
on cruise control now. I just gotta keep going; I'm swinging well and I can do this. I can get in the 50s and do
something pretty special." Obviously, I didn't think 55.

Next, I go to the par 5 12th and hit a great drive and
put it 35 feet from the hole from 210, hit a good putt that
almost goes in, and tap in for the birdie. I went par on #13,
and #14. I missed an eight-foot putt on 14 for a birdie and
thought, "You can't be doing that on a day like today." I
was being positive. I didn't shake my head or anything. I
just thought, "You don't miss a putt like that. Just hunker
down right here." So I go to the 15th hole and there's
water all down the left side. It was 337 over water to the
green, and while a lot of people might lay up, I said, "I've
got my foot on the pedal. I'm swinging well and there's
no reason I shouldn't hit a drive on the green." So I hit
a driver, a high cut, and put it on the green about 35 feet
from the cup . . . and I hit a great putt and it ended up at
the bottom of the cup. And I thought to myself, "I think
I'm in the 50s now."

SAUL: That was an eagle, 337 over water. And then sinking a 35-foot putt, you've got to be feeling good.

ALEXANDER: Yeah, I was feeling great. Everyone has a different game. My game is power. So, I said, "Don't be afraid and play away from that. Take it head-on." No great player has ever shot a great score by playing scared. There were a few shots I was hesitant on during that day, but toward the end of the round I got into such a zone, I knew I couldn't mess up on those last four holes. I made the 35-foot putt on #15 and right then, when it came off the putter face, I said, "Yes."

I hit a perfect 340-yard drive on #16 right down the middle, put my second shot right behind the pin, six feet from the hole. At that point I was one hundred percent sure I was going to birdie in. . . . I'm so locked in that nothing could distract me from doing that. I go to the 17th, I'm not talking to anyone at this point. Grant is not talking to me. The other two guys in the group, I barely talked to them all round. They knew what I was doing and kind of left me to do my thing. I go to #17, a par 3, 150 yards. I hit a pitching wedge, a high cut, and put it about six feet from the hole and putt in dead center to the cup. And when I get to #18, I know I'm 15 under par. Grant's not talking to me. He doesn't know what to say. I hit another great drive down the right side, and as I'm chipping I'm thinking, "If I make this shot, I will have the lowest score ever in golf." And I told myself contact was the biggest thing there. I knew I had to hit it solid to give it some sort of chance. I gave it a good ride. And I had a three-foot putt for a birdie. I'd be lying if I said I didn't feel a little bit tense on that last putt. I'd been putting great all day, so I just told myself, "Whatever happens, just release the putter head." And I put a pretty good stroke on it and it went in dead center. And I thought, "Holy cow, that was dead crazy." I got a little light-headed, because when you start thinking about it, it was crazy . . . out-of-body for sure.

SAUL: Well, a couple of things come to mind for me. One of them is, you are obviously a very good golfer. We always say that a good score indicates ability. It also appears that it helped that Grant was there. Maybe it helped that you listened to the message from Janice. The bottom line, Alexander, is you are a player. And one of the things to take away from the experience is, "That's who I am." When you don't overthink it, or over-effort, you can really score. I love the fact that you said, "I feel good about my swing and I'm just going to keep doing this."

I tell my clients that the mind is like this amazing supercomputer and you are the boss. You are response-able to put good programs on that computer. Good programs relate to how we think and how we feel. Right thinking is simple. It's what you were doing. It's knowing your strengths, knowing you are a long hitter, knowing you are swinging great, and thinking, "just keep doing it."

From the mental point of view, creating good focus, good feeling, and good attitude helps us to excel.

Good focus is knowing who you are, knowing your strength, and trusting your game. I work a lot with my clients on what I call "conscious breathing." It supports **good feeling** and it keeps people in the present. When we get anxious, we're usually thinking about the future — "Don't miss the next shot," "Don't slice," "Don't do _____" . . .

that's the future. How do I get it back to the present? Breathe. Experience this breath . . . and then the next breath. If you do regular breath training away from the golf course, then you can build up enough habit strength so that when you're under pressure, you just take a breath and it slips you back into the now — back into the good feeling zone. But to do that, you have to do the "home-work." You have to work with breathing on a regular basis.

And the big thing with **good attitude** is under-standing that if the goal is to be the best I can be, then whatever comes up I've got to *use it*. If you don't *use it* then *it can use you*. By that I mean, if you are hitting the ball well, acknowledge it. Say, "That's me." It builds confidence. If one hits one off-line, using it is saying, "That's not me," releasing tension or negativity, taking a breath, and refocusing on the positive. That's pretty much what you did after missing that birdie putt on #14.

I asked three retired NHL hockey players, all former clients and now keen golfers, if and how they were applying the mental training we worked on to improve their hockey performance, to improve their golf game (see Chapter 13). They said some interesting things. One player mentioned he found the breathing release technique especially useful after he made a poor shot. He said it helped to change irritation into inspiration, to focus on the positive, and stay in the moment . . . just as you did on #11 and on #14. And, as you said in our earlier discussion, "When I start thinking about not disappointing the sponsor — or any of that stuff — it's tensing, and it takes me out of the present moment."

One last thing, Alexander, I often ask golfers to pick an animal that would give them the feelings they'd want to have when they were playing their best. Alexander, what would you choose?

ALEXANDER: I would say a shark. Sharks are not malicious or evil; they hunt according to the laws of nature. Yeah, I would consider myself kind of like a shark . . . a great white shark. I have a killer instinct when I'm on the golf course — and that shuts off when I come off the golf course.

SAUL: When I ask elite athletes like you, 99 percent choose predators. What is the difference between the golfer who is the predator and the golfer who is the prey?

ALEXANDER: The golfers who are the prey let results control their lives. Obviously, it's understood results are important in every sport. But the prey are the people in the sporting world who let the results control their lives. They can't shut off the results. They play cautious, afraid to make a mistake, to lose out.

SAUL: Agreed. I think the big difference between the golf predator and the golf prey is that the golf predator steps out into the course to make something happen. The thinking is, "I'm going to put this ball there." Of course, they are playing for score, but their focus is making the shot. They have the eye of the tiger.

In contrast, in the back of the prey golfer's consciousness is an anxious feeling and the thought "Don't miss, don't make a mistake." Like you said, the result — the score — is controlling them. That takes us back to love and fear, and thinking, "I love to play this game," "I love to strike the ball." The shark loves to hunt. They just go for it. Alexander, on that 55-day, you were the predator. You felt strong, positively focused, and you were hunting . . . birdies.

There are a number of things Rhein and Alexander share in creating their remarkable scores of 55. For starters, both golfers were playing a recreational round.

- Both felt calm at the start.
- Neither felt pressured.
- Both were feeling good: Rhein had a country music tune running through his head the entire round that helped him to stay loose; and Alexander had young Grant with him, whom he was coaching on how to play the course, and Grant's presence was relaxing.
- Both got off to excellent starts. Both were 10 under (26) after nine holes.
- Both were putting great. Both thought they couldn't miss.
- Both had the feeling they were swinging well and were committed to doing more of the same.
- Both were trusting their swings and NOT making adjustments.
- Both believed they could do no wrong and made the shots they went for. There was no doubting.
- Both said they were having fun.
- Both consciously thought, "Don't rush this."
- Both let go of any negativity and excessive mental chatter. (They were playing with Gallwey's Mind 2. Mind 1 was relatively quiet.)

On the last nine holes, when they encountered some adversity, they "used it" to challenge themselves *in a positive way* to refocus and reaffirm. Rhein describes saving par on #15 but missing a birdie opportunity, and knowing he was going to birdie the last three holes, which he did. Similarly, Alexander missed a birdie putt on #14 and "used it" to refocus and reaffirm. He then scored an eagle #15 and affirmed he was going to birdie the last three holes, which he did.

What can we learn from Rhein's and Alexander's experience? One simple but important thing is, go out to play to *enjoy* the experience. If you can, allow yourself to get into that *good feeling* place. Respect yourself. Breathe easy and take your time. *Feel* your game and trust your swing. Do NOT overthink your game and make repeated adjustments. Whatever comes up, *use it* — release the negatives. Think positive. Know/feel you can make the shot. Allow yourself to play. If you do, you will perform better and enjoy the experience more.

MORE EXCEPTIONAL GOLF –
THOUGHTS FROM THE PGA TOUR'S SUB-60 CLUB

On June 10, 1977, **Al Geiberger** shot a 13-under 59 at the Danny Thomas Memphis Classic, in Memphis, Tennessee, becoming the first golfer to break 60 on the PGA Tour. Geiberger hit every fairway and every green and had only 23 putts. Of his achievement, Geiberger said, "When I initially shot it, I thought if I can do it, then anybody can do it. I didn't understand how hard it is to do. When someone gets close to a 59, they tend to run out of holes." Geiberger's immaculate ball-striking was complemented by even better putting. He pitched in from 30 yards for an eagle on his 10th hole, but much of his record score was on account of his fine putting (nine birdie putts outside 10 feet). Ten under with six holes to play, Geiberger made pars on #13 and #14. Geiberger remembered saying, "I had made two pars in a row, but I was hitting it better than I ever had in my life. My coach at Southern Cal, Stan Wood, used to say I was too conservative a player. He wanted me to be more aggressive. I thought, 'Now's the time to do it. If I screw up, it's Stan's fault.' I drove it right down the middle, hit it on the green, and made about a 10-footer. The gallery started yelling '59.' I hadn't thought of it. You don't count your score when you're shooting a good round. That's the kiss of death." Geiberger birdied #16, then sank a nine-foot birdie at #17. He faced an eight-footer on

#18 to shoot 59 — and made it. Reflecting on the experience years later, Geiberger summarized it: "I was in the zone."[4]

Annika Sorenstam is the only woman to shoot a sub-60 round on the LPGA Tour. Here's some of what Annika had to say about her 59 at Moon Valley, Arizona, in 2001: "I always believed I could birdie every hole. Growing up in Sweden we had something called Vision 54 . . . kind of a mental vision [program] as to how to play really good golf. It always talked about what it would feel like to hit every green. What it would feel like to make every putt. So, the question is, why can't you do it in one round? I always believed that it was possible. When I woke, I could feel something was going to happen. You only experience these feelings once or twice in your lifetime."

Annika recalled that her warm-up on the range and the putting green wasn't anything unusual: "I warmed up for an hour and 15 minutes. I don't remember hitting it exceptionally well on the range. I don't remember rolling more putts on the putting green. And I don't remember feeling anything particular in the mindset. It was like a normal Friday, round two."

However, when she began the round, she did something she had never done before. She birdied the first eight holes. She reported that was when she began to feel nervous. She said, "I felt uncomfortable because you start thinking and worrying, 'I don't want to jeopardize this. I don't want to ruin what I have done and what's happening here. I'm on track to birdie every hole.' That's when I realized this is pretty special. And when I got to the 9th tee, I said to my caddie, 'I'm so nervous, I'm so out of my comfort zone I just need to make par.' And I made par on #9. . . . And I walked to the 10th hole and I was feeling better. And I said to my caddie, 'I'm ready for more birdies.'" And she birdied the next four holes.

As she played the back nine, Annika noticed the crowd building. She reported trying to focus, to stay calm out there, to relate to her caddie like it was a normal Friday, but clearly it wasn't. On this super round, she missed one fairway, hit 18 greens and made 13 birdies.

Reflecting on the experience, Annika said, "Shooting 59 ranks pretty high. To be able to set history, to be the first [female player] to break 60. When I had this vision for so long, people looked at me and said you're crazy. But just to be able to prove that, and also to prove to myself, what I had worked so hard for."[5]

Jim Furyk, commenting on his 58 at Travelers Tournament in 2016, like Annika, noted that his warm-up wasn't exceptional. He remarked that he adjusted his swing: "I tried to kind of shorten it up a little today. And honestly, right from the go it was easy. Everything was going right at the flag . . . and I kind of put it on cruise and tried to stay out of my own way mentally."

Jim had previously shot a 59 at Conway Farms in 2013. Comparing these two remarkable rounds, Jim said, "Well, I had the 'here we go again feeling.' Turning the front nine, I had 8 under there, and I was 8 under on the front nine here today. I remember the mental battle, the grind. I kind of got off to a good start on the second side at Conway as well. So, I'm hitting it well; I'm putting well. It's try to find a way to stay out of your own way, really. Don't let any thoughts leak in. I left the first putt a little short at #17 and had to grind a little left to righter, but for the most part I think I hit every fairway and every green today. It was tougher conditions than Conway but a little smoother round of golf today."[6]

David Duval's 59 at the Bob Hope Classic in 1999 started with three birdies and made the turn at 28. He stated, "Breaking 60 was more important to me than winning the golf tournament. Maybe that's the wrong thing to say, but I thought, 'You are not going to have too many of these opportunities,' so I wanted to break 60 at that point. The most stressful and nervous was my second putt on #17. I was most nervous on that putt because I had to make that putt to have an opportunity to break 60."[7] He made the putt and moved to 18 with the opportunity to do something nobody had ever done. He had to eagle the last hole to come in under 60, and he did.

Scottie Scheffler, on his 59 at Northern Trust in 2020, said, "Today was a really good day on the course. I got off to a good start and made a bunch of birdies on the front nine and some key ups and downs at the beginning of the round that kind of got me rolling, and freed me up a little bit. The momentum just kept going. I never really lost momentum today which was nice. A lot of times when you're playing really well sometimes you can lose that momentum toward the end of the round. You can have a little hiccup here or there but the momentum stayed the whole time. I made a lot of nice putts.

"Was I nervous on the four-foot putt on #18? Yeah, you don't really get a putt for 59 often, so I was quite nervous over the putt. But that's nothing new. I get nervous over every shot. That's playing competitive golf."

When asked if he recalled any key shots, Scottie replied, "I would say the ones at the beginning. It's hard when you are sitting outside of the cut line at the beginning of the day knowing that you have to shoot 2 or 3 under just to make the cut. Getting off to a good quick start was definitely key and I just kept that momentum going the whole day."[8]

Here's the account of **Adam Hadwin** on his 59 at the CareerBuilder Challenge in La Quinta, California, in 2017. Hadwin's excellent round consisted of six consecutive birdies on the front nine, and five in a row on the back nine. On the 412 yard, par 4, 18th hole, his approach went long and left, leaving Hadwin to chip across the green, which ended three feet from the hole. Standing over the short putt he had to make to shoot a 59, Hadwin said he was worried about what would happen if he missed. "I thought to myself, if you miss a straight three-foot putt uphill to shoot 59, you'll never live it down. Then I thought, I had to forget about that and focus on my routine." He said he tried to run the same putt routine, just like one he's made thousands of times. Reflecting, Hadwin commented he was very conscious that, in some respects, this wasn't like any other three-foot putt he'd made, but in other respects, it was exactly like every putt he'd made in practice rounds or in other tournament rounds. Hadwin said, "I just thought about what I always do and visualized the ball going in the hole. I think what gave me the most confidence is that I knew exactly what I needed to do."[9]

The similarities in many of these extraordinary sub-60 rounds are: getting off to an excellent start — shooting in the 20s at the turn and realizing something "special" is possible . . . having a good feeling — the iron play being sharp, hitting every green, and the putting having eyes. Several golfers commented that they struggled to manage their emotions and stay out of their own way mentally.

Another 59-rounder, **Chip Beck**, who shot a 59 at the Sunrise Country Club in Las Vegas in 1999, summarized it nicely when he said, "It seemed like every time I turned around, I was hitting a good shot right at the pin. And that's what it takes to shoot 59. And, I don't care where you're playing, you have to make the putts."[10]

Improvements in fitness and power and developments in golf technology (clubs and balls) have led to people hitting longer and straighter. All of which suggests we will no doubt be seeing an increasing number of golfers joining the remarkable sub-60 club in the next few years.

MANAGING EMOTIONS: THE GOOD, THE BAD, AND THE UGLY

The Good

When the good feeling is there: On winning the Valspar Golf Tournament (and shortly after shooting 59 at La Quinta), Adam Hadwin was asked about winning his first PGA Tour event. "I think, more than anything else, it's the continued hard work and finding my way out here. I understand the golf courses a little more; I understand what it takes to win out there a little better. I put myself in a position in the first couple of years to have a chance to win some golf tournaments and I hadn't been able to get it done. And I think that all led to Valspar. I felt comfortable. I felt like I belonged out there, and that's a good feeling to have out there."

The Bad and the Ugly

When the good feeling is not there: After a round at the 2020 Masters, Hadwin, asked about his performance, said, "It was just below awful. My iron play was just awful, terrible. I'm not sure if I hit one good iron shot today. It was extremely disappointing" and "I just hit terrible. . . . I'm about as lost as I've ever been hitting the irons. Too many shots are going not where I'm looking."

Hadwin went on to say that he had good iron shots in the practice rounds but that in the tournament round "I felt lost . . . a couple off line on the front nine kind of didn't do what I wanted them to do, and then I just start questioning a little bit, start thinking . . . and the next thing you know you're kind of missing everything."[11]

Managing emotions is a critical part of consistent good play. And clearly, good feelings support good thinking and good play. Bad feelings do just the opposite.

"Choking" is a psycho-physical phenomenon that athletes in all sports experience under pressure. They become anxious, and their anxiety triggers fight-or-flight chemicals, which flow through their bodies causing their breathing to shorten, their muscles to tense, and their touch, flow, and confidence to disappear. Golfers are certainly not immune to choking. Effective solutions to "choking" are mastering conscious breathing, the release reflex, positive self-talk, and positive imagery. And while choking and the yips may be somewhat different, both situations are benefitted by lowering anxiety, shifting consciousness to the breath, beta to alpha, and tuning in to feeling and flow.

> "A lot of guys who have never choked have
> never been in the position to do so."
> – Tom Watson

SECTION FOUR
RIGHT ATTITUDE

"Golf is a game in which attitude of mind counts for
incomparably more than mightiness of muscle."
– Arnold Haultain

"A bad attitude is worse than a bad swing."
– Payne Stewart

With the right attitude, almost anything is possible. Remember, attitude is a matter of choice and *you* are the chooser.

CHAPTER EIGHT

Commitment

"Your success only makes you more motivated to be
better. . . . My lowest score here is 64 and I'd love to better
that. I want to try to be the best golfer in the world."
— Rory McIlroy

Success begins with motivation. Motivation is what moves us to action. It's about desire, commitment, and goals. As I said at the outset, goals work. Setting goals clarifies direction and increases success in life. It's about putting things in priority and clarifying purpose. But it's not enough to simply set a goal and repeat your goal statement — you have to do the work. Some athletes set excellent goals for themselves but are simply not willing to follow through with the day-to-day actions to make their goals a reality.

Commitment is the willingness to pay the price and do what's necessary to get the result you want. In golf that means doing the day-to-day physical, technical, and mental training needed to build up your fitness, technical prowess, competitive focus, emotional control, and the positive attitude required to excel. Consistent hard work is an expression of commitment, and it's essential to success. Many past golf "stars" offer the same advice for a young golfer wanting to excel at the highest level.

Here are three PGA Tour Champions on commitment and the push to be the best:

Lee Trevino: "When you want to be the best, you gotta do something extra. You can't just do the same thing everybody else is doing. All the great ones do that. I out practiced them. The better I did, the more I'd like to see it, and the more I practiced."[1]

Tiger Woods: "No matter how good you get, you can always be better — and that's the exciting part. . . . It's something you have to find from within. You have to keep pushing yourself from within. It's not about what other people think or say. It's about what you want to accomplish and do you want to go out there and be prepared to beat everyone you play or face."[2]

Matt Kuchar: "Even if you finish No. 1 in the world, and Tiger Woods has done this, you can still probably get better."[3]

Commitment is the willingness to put in the necessary time and effort to excel. Willingness involves making a choice. The following statement by Forrest Gregg, an NFL Hall of Fame player and football coach, can apply to us all: "To be a winner one must be totally committed. . . . Total commitment means being willing to do whatever is necessary to become successful. One must be willing to work hard, to push themselves physically until it hurts. . . . To be a winner one must be willing to make sacrifices. . . . If you want to be a winner you will give up anything that does not help you become better at your sport. All athletes are not endowed with the same physical abilities. One can, and many before you have, overcome a lack of ability with extra effort. These people are totally committed."[4]

As golf legend Jack Nicklaus has said, "You have to love something and have a passion for it to be disciplined. My commitment was purely to golf."[5]

COMMITMENT = USING IT

I mentioned this in an earlier chapter, and it is worth repeating: *If your goal is to be the best golfer you can be, then whatever comes up, learn to "use it."* If you don't use it, *it can use you*. It's important to learn how to *use it*, whatever the situation or challenge confronting you. If you have a good shot or a good round, *use it* to reaffirm your ability and build your confidence. Think, "That's me!" If you have a poor performance, *use it* to improve your process — release any negativity, clear the screen on your mental computer, breathe in energy, and refocus on something positive.

> "I kept telling myself this word, process.
> Focus on my process, don't care about the
> result." — Rory McIlroy

The practice of using it involves seeing the positive even in an undesirable result and *using it* to stimulate you to improve your practice and tournament performance. This is important! I repeat: The process of *using it* in negative situations is about activating the release reflex — releasing tension and negativity, breathing in energy, and refocusing on the positive (e.g., on training to improve your focus, feeling, or technique; on seeing yourself effectively executing skills on the course; on working out to become more powerful, like a tiger or eagle; and on doing more of what it takes to become a winner).

Just imagine hitting the ball well, straight down the fairway. It looks like a good shot. However, when you get to the ball, you notice it's lying in a deep divot. Seeing the ball mired in the divot, a golfer who is upset, who thinks something like, "Unbelievable, just my luck . . . a good shot and a horrible lie. How am I supposed to score from here?" is letting the situation *use* him or her. The negativity, upset, and dis-ease experienced is inclined to make a good next shot less likely.

Contrast that with the golfer committed to *using it*, who after assessing the situation is more inclined to think, "Okay, here's a chance to make a good shot from a bad lie." Remember, you get more of what you think about, and you are the boss. You can't always control the situation, but you can control your reaction to it. Winners "use" everything. Losers let the situation use them.

Jim Nelford had been a two-time NCAA All-American and a Canadian Amateur Champion before joining the PGA Tour, where he experienced some impressive finishes (and made 35 straight cuts) before being injured in a waterskiing accident. Jim's right arm was severely sliced by a propeller blade and, unable to play, he was granted a PGA exemption. He was struggling to get back to competitive form when I consulted with him. I recall walking the course with Jim while he was playing in the LA Open. He wasn't playing at the level he had been prior to the accident, and he wasn't getting the breaks. At one point I recall his hitting a solid shot down the fairway, only to have the ball end up in a bad lie. When he saw the lie, he simply shook his head, then he smiled, took a breath and a smooth practice swing, stepped up to the ball, and played a good shot.

Winners are not free from disappointment, fear, and negativity. Like everyone else, they experience uncertainty and doubt. It's just that they don't dwell on it. Instead, they *use it* to refocus and stay on the power channel. Winners use everything.

> "Golf is about how well you accept, respond
> to, and score with your misses much more so
> than it is a game of your perfect shots."
> – Dr. Bob Rotella

It's been said, "Golf is not a game of perfect." We've all witnessed a golfer making an errant shot and then getting upset. In most cases, the emotion makes the next shot more difficult. When that errant shot does happen, my advice is *use it* as follows; release any tension or frustration with the release reflex, breathe in some positive energy, take aim at your intended target, then take a full swing and imagine/ visualize the ball flying directly to your target. Then say to yourself, "That's who I am."

I recall watching Vijay Singh do something very similar on his way to winning the Canadian Open in 2004. After hitting a drive a little too far to his right, Singh stood there for a moment, took a breath, sited his target, took a full swing, and then appeared to visualize the imaginary ball flying to the target. Thereafter, I believe he reaffirmed his prowess, saying something to himself, like "That's who I am."

Your ability to release the negative and turn an errant shot into a positive experience will give you more consistency and impact.

Here are a few more suggestions about how to *use it* in each of the following situations. When good things are happening, when you've had a good round, or when you are tuned in to practice and executing skills well — *use it* — take a breath or two, acknowledge yourself, think "That's who I am." The tiger, cheetah, or eagle is hunting. Take another breath (or two) and get ready to hunt again. *Using it* when things are good builds confidence.

When you've had a poor round, when you've lost focus and duffed shots, or when you felt tired, weak, or nervous — take a breath, think "That's not me," see yourself making adjustments and improving your physical or mental training process . . . and get ready to hunt again.

Something I Did Well

An expression of commitment and *using it* can occur in your post-competition analysis. Win or lose, after every round, *first* think of one or two things that you did well. Then, and only then, think of just one thing you can improve. Working on increasing your strengths and improving those areas that need improvement is a way to grow your competitive success. Human nature is often to focus first on what one did poorly. Watch out for that trap. It leads to negative thinking and undermines confidence. Instead, always focus first on what you did well.

I frequently speak to management, coaching groups, and sports teams on winning, teamwork, and leadership. I routinely ask the groups to rank five key qualities in terms of their relationship to team success. The five qualities are talent, leadership, strategy, commitment, and chemistry. Over the years almost every group has rated commitment as *number 1*. An important part of commitment is *using it*.

Modeling is one of the most powerful forms of learning. One school of thought states if you want to improve at something, anything, get involved with people (athletes) who are more successful than you. Observing their focus, determination, work ethic, and ability to *use it* can provide some positive modeling.

> "I'm not even close to Rory McIlroy or Jordan [Spieth]. I just need to practice more and hopefully soon I'll be able to play to the same level they do."[6] — Hideki Matsuyama

Two additional expressions of commitment are perseverance and discipline.

Perseverance is the quality of a winner. Calvin Coolidge said, "Nothing in this world can take the place of persistence. Talent will not; nothing is more common than unsuccessful men with talent. Genius will not; unrewarded genius is almost a proverb. Education will not; the world is full of educated derelicts. Persistence and determination alone are omnipotent. The slogan Press On! has solved and always will solve the problems of the human race."[7]

There are many excellent examples of athletes who were told they did not have the "right stuff" or individuals who overcame serious injury and illness and, despite the odds, persisted and ultimately achieved at the highest level.

I learned the benefits of persistence early in my career. I recall telephoning the head coach of one NHL team and leaving several messages with his secretary. When he didn't return my call, I called again and again. I must have called and left six or seven messages, but still there was no return call. Finally, on my seventh or eighth call he picked up the phone. When I said, "It's Dr. Saul Miller speaking," his response was a somewhat sarcastic, "Well, you certainly are persistent." To which I replied, "Persistence is the quality of a winner," and added, "You expect your players to persist in the game, don't you?"

His mood shifted. He laughed and said, "Yes, I certainly do," and then, "What can I do for you?" I replied that I wanted an opportunity to meet with him to explain what I could do to help the team be more successful. Somewhat unenthusiastically, he agreed to an appointment. We met in his office several days later. Shortly thereafter, he referred several players to me. When I began work with the team it was mid-season, and they had won only three of their previous 21 games. The team's performance picked up; they made it into the playoffs, kept winning, and went all the way to the Stanley Cup finals. What I find especially interesting about the story is how my comment "Persistence is the quality of a winner" appeared to open a door to our meeting. It literally changed his thinking from "This guy is a nuisance" to "This person is determined." My perseverance came from a sincere belief that I had something useful to contribute and from my commitment to make a positive difference. The coach sensed my determination and an opportunity was presented. (And the result suggests my involvement did contribute to an improvement in performance.)

Winners are positive. They believe in themselves. They believe in the goal they are working toward and the process that will get them there. Their belief stimulates them to act and persevere.

Discipline is another characteristic of commitment and winning. The legendary NCAA basketball coach Bobby Knight sees discipline and commitment as one quality. "It has always been my thought that the most important single ingredient in success in athletics or life is discipline. I have many times felt that this word is the most ill-defined in our language. My definition of the word is this: Do what has to be done. When it has to be done. As well as it can be done. And, do it that way all the time."[8]

"A lot of my buddies also played golf, but when it came to going to the beach or on the boat and chasing girls, they usually went that way . . . and I went to the golf course."
— Mike Weir

Early Mental Coaching

Discipline can be coached, and that coaching can begin fairly early. The following is a golf example of some early mental coaching. I had a phone call from a woman who said, "My son, Matt, is a good golfer and he has some issues with controlling his emotions. Is that something you could help him with?" I replied that I do work with clients helping them to manage their emotions. That's when she informed me that her son was seven.

Matt was a bright youngster with lots of energy who didn't exactly sit still during our sessions. As I do with most of my young clients, I asked a parent (in this case, his mother) to sit in. And, as I also frequently do with young clients, I began the session by asking the parent how she hoped the meetings with me would be helpful for Matt. She explained, "When Matt makes a bad shot, he sometimes gets very upset — he cries, he shouts, and sometimes he even throws his golf clubs, all of which is unacceptable. He has been told by me and his father that this behavior is unacceptable. Officials from the golf club have also told him this." She continued, "Matt expresses some overt happiness when an opponent makes a bad shot, which he has been told is also unacceptable. We've told him he has to learn to behave better if he wants to continue to play golf."

I asked Matt what he thought about what his mother had said. He agreed that he gets upset when he makes a bad shot. With some prompting, he said he understood that to be a really good golfer he has to learn to be more calm. I explained to him that the reason he gets upset is that he really wants to do well. But getting upset like he does when things don't go as he would like is not acceptable golf behavior, and, most importantly, it is behavior that will make it harder for him to have a good next shot.

I asked Matt if he wanted to learn how to be calmer, just like PGA Tour golfers. He nodded that he did so we began training. I adapted my usual training process in consideration of Matt's age. First, I explained to him that the mind is like a mental supercomputer and that it was *his* mental computer. If he didn't like what he was thinking or feeling, he had to change the program. I said the first thing was learning how to take a couple of breaths and relax. We ran through a simple breathing exercise. I told Matt that he had to practice five minutes of relaxed (conscious) breathing every day. Next, I showed him how to use the release reflex. I had him make his muscles tense, then release the tension, and think "calm." I explained this was the way to change the program on his supercomputer. If he practiced this "calm reflex" when he felt angry or frustrated, he would be able to let go of the tension and frustration — and have the same control as a PGA golfer. Matt said he understood and would practice these techniques.

In our next session we reviewed the breathing-calming techniques, then I introduced a positive focusing exercise. I reminded Matt that the mind is like a mental supercomputer, that he was becoming a pretty good golfer, and that his job was to put positive thoughts on his mental computer. He said he understood and he would do that. "Okay then," I said, "Let's look at some good thoughts and good feelings that you can put on your mental computer that would help you to play some good golf." With a little prompting, Matt talked about feeling strong and relaxed, taking a breath, and then he mentioned some of the things his golf coach had taught him — pick a target; have a nice, smooth, slow backswing; and keep his head still as he was hitting the ball. I asked Matt, "What can you do when the shot you just made wasn't good and the ball doesn't go where you wanted it to go?" Again, with some prompting, he said, "I could take a breath, see the shot I wanted to make, and think, 'That's what I'll do next time.'"

"Okay, Matt," I replied, "these are very good thoughts that you can say to yourself. And I encourage you to practice thinking and saying them. It's important to practice good thinking just like you practice having a good golf swing." I added, "If you practice thinking these thoughts when you're practicing your golf shots, they will become habits and they will be there for you when you're competing." I then gave Matt four homework exercises.

1. Every day when you wake up in the morning and go to the bathroom to brush your teeth, look at your face in the mirror and say to yourself, "I am becoming a good golfer. I make lots of good shots. And I can be calm like a PGA golfer."

2. The second homework assignment was to practice his calm breathing exercise (at least once) every day, each time for five minutes.

3. The third homework assignment (which frankly was a little challenging for a seven-year-old) was that any time you notice yourself getting angry or frustrated, remember you are the boss of how you feel, so release tension, take a breath, and think, "Calm and strong."

4. The last homework exercise we went over involved creating and practicing a routine for each golf shot that consisted of taking a breath, seeing the shot he wanted to make, taking a practice swing to re-create the feeling he wanted to have to make that shot, aligning himself to the target, taking a breath, and making

a nice, smooth swing through the ball. And after the shot, taking another breath.

We had two more sessions over the next two months, and all reports were that Matt's golf demeanor and his play noticeably improved.

More good advice on coaching young golfers, from Nancy Lopez, a golf Hall of Famer — with 48 LPGA wins — a golf instructor, and parent. I asked Nancy what she would say to a serious young golfer about managing their mental game.

She replied, "Well, the way my dad put it to me one day, and he was pretty smart . . . he looked at me, and I was getting angry and I was young. And young people get angry because they want it to happen yesterday. And because he played golf, he knew that anger did not help me play better. So, his statement to me was, 'Do you want to shoot 39 or do you want to shoot 40?' And I said, 'I want to shoot 39.' And he said, 'Well, when you get mad like that you shoot 40.' And it was like, 'OK, he's right. I get angry and I shoot 40. And even though it's just one shot, I don't want to shoot 40. He always had an anecdote for feeling things like that. As a young person I got that. Instead of him saying, 'Don't get mad, don't get angry,' he put it to me that way, and I just related to that comment better than anything he probably could have said."

Nancy continued, "There's good anger and there's bad. You can get mad maybe doing something stupid, but you can't let that affect a shot. . . . My dad helped me realize that golf cannot control my life. That I had to go out there and enjoy it, otherwise I may as well quit. He was fun. He was a very positive man. He never put pressure on me. He let me learn the lessons that helped me love the game. And I think that's the big difference, because I think these days there's a lot of great young players on the Tour whose parents are obsessed with making them champions. You cannot fear failure, and I think lots of times they fear failure. And when their round is done, they get beat up verbally by a parent, or the parent makes them feel bad about one shot, or maybe they just didn't play that well.

"I never did that with my three girls. They played all sports . . . and watching them play softball and basketball and track, I always used my method of teaching them, just like my dad did. And if it was one of those times when I sensed one of them thought she could have done better, she never saw that emotion from me. I would go behind a building to hide my feelings before I would express any kind of negative emotion that she would ever see. I just don't think that was good. I never saw that from my dad."

When I commented that aggressive, hypercritical, negative parents can push their children away from their sport, Nancy replied, "Absolutely. I just know that my dad got the most out of me by encouraging me, not disciplining me or making me feel guilty or sad. My daughters played team sports, not individual sports like I did, where you can beat yourself up. They were really good softball players and there were days when they said, 'Mom, I can't believe we can't be better.' And I said, 'Sweetie, you're not the only one on the team.' I always looked at them and said, 'Did you give a hundred percent?' And they would say, 'Yes, ma'am,' and I would say, 'That's all you can do. There are days when it is not going to be perfect . . . so when you walk off the golf course and you know you gave a hundred percent, then walk off the golf course with pride.'"9

And some more advice for playing golf with your young son or daughter — *keep it simple and keep it fun.*

At the 2020 PNC Father-Son Championship in Orlando, Florida, Tiger Woods, playing with his 11-year-old son, Charlie, was asked if the cameras and tournament surroundings were a distraction to Charlie.

Tiger replied, "It was the way we planned it. It was he and I. We got into our little world. It was pure golf. See the shot . . . and execute it. And we did that."10

It's not surprising that Tiger would coach his son to get into their little golf world. Years before, young Tiger was taught the importance of narrow focus and not being distracted by what's happening around him. It's said that when he was very young, Tiger's father, Earl Woods, would often bang clubs and make loud noises when his son was in mid-swing, to prepare him for distractions he might experience in competition.[11] Father-son coaching lessons in coping with distraction is apparently generational in the Woods family.

Winning is about sustained focus. To achieve success, maintain a practice focus on what is relevant. And, when you play, tune out all those stimuli (however alluring) that could be seen as distracting, pressuring, or irrelevant.

> "To give yourself the best possible chance of playing to your potential, you must prepare for every eventuality. That means practice."
> – Seve Ballesteros

In order to trust your swing, you must practice, practice, and practice. I encourage you to work to create a more natural swing — one that feels centered, balanced, and fluid — that feels right to you. Developing a natural swing enables you to turn off swing-mechanic-thinking, and trust and feel the swing is there. It is the basis of consistency and confidence that we explore in the next chapter.

TRAINING EXERCISES

1. Review your long- and short-term golf goals. On a 7-point scale, rate how committed you are to making them happen, where:

1 represents "very weakly committed" and 7 represents "very strongly committed."

2. Make a list of some things you can and are going to do physically, technically, and mentally to become a better golfer. Review the list — then get to work.

3. Choose one thing about golf that has been "using you" and getting you down, and think of how you can *use it* to be a more effective golfer.

4. In practice, consciously work on good swing mechanics. When you play, consciously work at trusting and feeling the swing/stroke.

CHAPTER NINE

Confidence

"Confidence is king in golf."
– Jason Dufner

Confidence is key to a winning attitude, and confidence is basic to how we perform. The word confidence comes from the Latin word *confidere*, meaning "to trust." The golfer who is confident trusts his or her focus, feelings, and swing or stroke. He or she believes that they can and will perform well. Rhein Gibson, in describing his remarkable round of 55 (see Chapter 7) said, "I felt invincible, almost like I knew when I was standing over some of the putts, I just knew that it was going to go in the hole. It was a momentous round. I made a birdie, I made an eagle, I made a birdie and another birdie. My performance was always there."[1] That "knowing" makes it more likely one will excel. The two most basic ways to build confidence are through success and preparation.

Confidence breeds success: After winning the British Open, Collin Morikawa was asked about being a rookie and winning a Major links tournament on his first try. How did he overcome that? Morikawa said, "You try not to listen to everything when it's your rookie year, it's your debut. If you do, you do, and sometimes it gets to people.

"At the Travelers Championship, my third PGA Tour event, I heard Brooks [Koepka] say that he's there to win. He said, when he first turned pro, he was there to make cuts, and then to make the top 30s, then top 20s, and then top 10s . . . and from that day I switched to 'Lets go out and win.' [And win Morikawa has, with two Major victories in the fewest starts (eight) in over 80 years.]

"By the time I was in the PGA Championship last year, I had already played in events with all these guys, all the big-name guys, and it was like a normal event. So I come out this week; I'm not worried about playing against everyone else. I'm just trying to learn the golf course. And learning a links course is tough because there are so many slopes and I like to know everything, every little detail possible."[2]

When Morikawa was asked, after his strong final round at the British Open, "At what point did you start to believe this would be your day?" Morikawa replied, "The time I woke up." Then he added, "I never felt it was my tournament until I tapped in that birdie putt on 18 . . . because anything could happen."[3]

Rick Sessinghaus is a PGA instructor and mental coach who has worked with Morikawa since Collin was eight years old. When Sessinghaus was asked, "What was Collin's mindset coming into the Open, especially it being his debut appearance?" he replied, "Well, I think he even said that in the interviews, 'It's to win.' And every week his goal is to win. And his preparation needs to follow in line with that. Preparation is everything."[4]

"Confidence is such a precious and
fragile thing." – David Duval

After winning the Lotte LPGA Championship, Lydia Ko commented, "When I'm hitting it with confidence and an aggressive mindset, that's when I hit it the best and play the best, because I'm more free and I'm controlling it less. I think I was being less tentative and sticking to my game plan. If it was a tough driving hole, I hit it even more aggressively. Things just clicked, and I don't mean in a technical way, but between the ears."[5]

Scott Shelton, a former NCAA and PGA pro mentioned that when he was a young professional Mark Calcavecchia talked with him about playing aggressively. He said Mark's philosophy was he would win all his money in a few events, so for that reason he was going to fire at every flag and try to birdie every hole. He knew that some weeks it would not work and he would play poorly, but he was willing to take that chance to win. As a young pro this was eye-opening to me and a much different attitude than just playing to make cuts.

Scott also mentioned that for a couple of years he worked with Phil Blackmar. He said, "Phil had stopped playing and was doing TV at the time for the Golf Channel. I would go down to his house and stay for a couple days and we worked on everything, technique, strategies, and the mental game. Phil always talked about keeping your foot on the gas. When you get 2 under, work to get 3, and when you get 3, work to get 4. In my opinion this is a concept that is tough to teach. The guys who have managed to have long PGA tour careers are really good at this. I believe this is what truly separates players . . . not physical skills because we all had those . . . but the confidence and aggressiveness."

Sometimes it takes the right situation to bring out that aggressiveness. At the 2019 Valero, Corey Conners got the last of Valero's Monday qualifying spots by winning a six-man playoff. He went on to win the tournament (one of only five Monday qualifiers in PGA Tour history to hoist the trophy at week's end). Reflecting on the experience, Corey said, "You kind of have to have that aggressive mindset on the Monday qualifiers to give yourself lots of birdie chances. And I think our plan for that week after Monday qualifying was to keep that up. Be really aggressive ... and give myself some good birdie chances. And I was able to do that. I definitely think it helped. I gained a lot of confidence from that Monday, having success and being aggressive and giving myself good chances."[6]

SUCCESS BUILDS CONFIDENCE

In this chapter, there are some cross-sport examples illustrating how success builds confidence. That message is certainly applicable to golf.

Markus Naslund, a former NHL All-Star winger and captain of the Vancouver Canucks, made an interesting comment about confidence. Markus told me, "When I am playing well and scoring goals, I look forward to every shift. I think positive. I feel like I can score every time I get on the ice. When I haven't scored in several games, I notice that I start thinking more negatively. Thoughts like 'How long will this scoring drought last?' start creeping into my mind." He added that these thoughts vanish quickly after he scores a goal or two.[7]

The experience Markus describes is common. After performing well, people feel more confident, and that surge of confidence has a positive influence on their performance. The trick is to learn to create those positive, confident feelings even before experiencing a positive result. Doing that increases the probability of the desired result happening.

The following is an account of a golf client who had been struggling and how he regained his feeling, touch, and confidence. Bruce was a good young golfer. He had been an all-star in college. The success he had in college carried over when he began his pro career on a developmental tour. However, after a couple of months on the pro circuit, Bruce telephoned and said, "I'm in a slump. For the past month, I'm missing greens. I'm not getting up and down, and my putting isn't sharp." He asked me if I could help him regain his confidence and his scoring touch.

I listened to him, took a breath, and replied, "Bruce, you're a good golfer. In golf, like in all other sports, athletes sometimes experience 'dry spells,' where they just don't get a break. In golf, it's when greens are not holding, there's the occasional misread, varying green-speeds, putts just go by the rim or lip-out. Worrying about it makes it worse. I'll recommend a few things you can do to start scoring again: The first thing is to remember to relax and breathe. It will help you to feel calm and strong. Do a 10-to-15-minute breathing session every day, and bring your conscious breathing awareness to the range and the golf course."

"Yeah, I'm doing some of that," he replied. "I do it most days before a round. And I often take a couple of breaths between shots."

"Okay, good," I replied. "The second thing is mental rehearsal. It is really helpful to *relax and imagine* those actions that come to mind when you think of playing your best." I advised Bruce to imagine playing golf as he had at times in the past when every part of his game felt on, when he was strong off the tee, hitting greens, putting with touch, and "scoring." And I gave Bruce a number of examples: "Get in touch with your core and imagine swinging smooth and hitting long and straight off the tee. Imagine feeling balanced and making great approach shots with the ball stopping two, three feet from the pin. Imagine playing out of trouble. Imagine reading the greens, having fine touch, and sinking putts." I continued, "When I say, 'Imagine this,' I don't mean just sitting there with your eyes closed and visualizing it. *Feel it.* Actually get up and take an imaginary swing. Imagine feeling calm and strong, having your comfortable, grooved swing, playing with confidence and ease, trusting your swing, and enjoying the challenge that golf is." Then I added, "Bruce, every day I want you to imagine 20 great approach shots and finishing with a birdie putt. Do you understand what I'm describing?"

Bruce replied that he understood, and that he would do the positive imagery. "And remember, Bruce, every time you have a negative or worrisome thought or image, release it — take a breath, feel calm and strong, and imagine/feel yourself taking a smooth swing, striking the ball well, and making the shot or sinking a putt."

Third, I told Bruce to actually practice on the range and around and on the green. "Work with your swing so that you feel balanced and comfortable and feel like you can trust your swing to send the ball where you want it to go. Focus and practice hitting targets on the range. Practice your chipping. Practice putting with touch and feel. Regarding putting practice, create a training routine. Here's a suggestion: Arrange six balls in a three-foot circle around the hole. See the line. Feel the putting stroke. Now make all six and repeat the process. It builds trust in your stroke, and that builds confidence. Then, go to six balls from five feet — make all six and do it twice. Then go to six balls from 10 feet, make as many as you can, do it twice, none finishing outside two feet. And then drop six balls from 20 to 30 feet, make as many as you can twice, none finishing outside six feet. Bruce, practice does make perfect, and it builds trust and confidence. That's true in every sport, especially golf.

"The fourth thing to remember — and it's important — is to know this in your bones and to say to yourself again and again, 'I am a good golfer. I read the game well. I have solid technique, a stroke I can feel and trust. I consistently hit greens (see it). And I'm a scorer. I can finish.' Bruce, that's who you are. You love the game. You work hard. You love to compete. Follow this advice and you will be fine."

When I spoke to Bruce two weeks later, he reported that the drought was over and he was playing with more feel and scoring again. He was back to playing with confidence.

Okay, reader, now let's go through the four steps as it relates to your game: 1, relax and breathe to regain composure. *Feel calm and strong.* 2, do some mental rehearsal — imagine yourself golfing great. Imagine and feel yourself playing with a smooth swing, striking the ball well. 3, actually practice every part of the game, with good technique so you can trust your swing and stroke, especially around and on the green. 4, know you are a good golfer. Know it, repeat it, feel it, and be it.

Recall Paul McGinley's comment (Section 2) that self-doubt occurs because one is too result-oriented and not in to the process and feeling of what they are doing: "You've got to create fun in what you are doing. It's the fun of the challenge. It's still focused. It's still driven. But you are not obsessed by the result. . . . You are in the moment."[8]

Range Play

A question I've been asked a number of times is "How can I feel as confident of my game on the golf course as I do on the range?"

For most golfers, there's obviously little consequence for mishits on the range. Consequently, golfers often feel more at ease on the range. Some feel better and hit better, which grows confidence. Second, golfers tend to approach shots differently on the range. Frequently, they don't go through their whole shot setup routine before each range shot as they might on the golf course. Third, if they should mishit balls on the range, they tend to be less upset and have less negative self-perception than when mishitting on the golf course.

Of course, some golfers are more dialed in, more focused, and play better on the golf course. However, if you are one of those golfers who wants to transfer better range confidence to the golf course, here are a few suggestions. Make a significant part of your range practice, especially before a round, as similar to course play as possible. To do that, first, practice on the range with definite purpose. Focus on setting a clear target for each range shot; second, approach each range shot with the same pre-shot routine/setup as you would on the golf course. And third, if your feel yourself playing with more angst and tension on the golf course where shots are consequential, work with the emotional management techniques outlined in Chapters 3, 4, 5, and 6 (conscious breathing, tension-release, positive self-talk, high-performance imagery) to have more emotional control in pressure situations.

Remember, people tend to perform under pressure as they previously did in pressure situations *unless* they overtrain themselves with emotional management techniques *away* from the pressure. In so doing, they build up enough "habit strength" that they can play with ease and confidence in pressure situations. Chris, a client, developed what I think is an effective confidence building range practice. First, he would hit a number of balls to work on improving specific mechanics. When he was satisfied with that process, he would switch to approaching each shot as he would if he was playing a round on the golf course. He would imagine teeing off (say on a long par 5 hole). To make the experience more like course play before striking the ball, Chris would run through his pre-shot routine. He would select a club (for example, his driver), pick a target spot, take a breath, and a smooth practice swing, then address the ball, take another breath, and tee off. Chris would then select another spot, choose a long iron or wood, run through his pre-shot routine, and take that shot. For his third shot on the imaginary hole, he would pick a target relatively close, take a wedge, run through his pre-shot routine, and hit a chip shot toward that target.

After making a successful approach shot, Chris would create another imaginary hole, select appropriate targets and clubs, and run through his full pre-shot routine each time, before taking a smooth swing and hitting the shot toward his target.

The number one answer to the question of what builds confidence is success — success playing golf well. But what if you haven't had success lately? What can you do to grow your confidence when you haven't been golfing at your best? The answer lies in *preparation*.

PREPARATION BUILDS CONFIDENCE

Preparation is the second key to building confidence. Looking up at a high mountain peak from the valley below, the task of climbing to the top may seem overwhelming. You may be unsure if you have the confidence and belief that you can do it. However, the task becomes less daunting if you break down the climb into steps and stages, with several elements to work on at each stage. With training, as you experience taking these steps and completing each stage, your confidence and belief that you can complete the climb will grow.

In climbing your golf mountain, work to achieve your golf goals.

Visualize yourself taking the necessary steps to build your confidence:

1. Improve your fitness so you feel strong and coordinated and you can trust your body. Quality fitness also enhances emotional management.
2. Work with your swing mechanics so you can feel centered, balanced, comfortable, and can trust your swing.
3. Do the breathing and release work so you feel calm and centered, and you can trust your emotions, especially in pressure situations.

> "Confidence is the most important single factor in this game, and no matter how great your natural talent, there is only one way to obtain it and sustain it: work." – Jack Nicklaus

SEPARATION BY PREPARATION

After winning the Superbowl, Russell Wilson, the quarterback of the Seattle Seahawks, related that one of the team's guiding principles was *separation by preparation.* "The way we prepare is what separates us from others."[9] It's a brilliant principle because it works both up and down. That is, you can separate yourself upwards from others by dedicating yourself to your physical, skill, and mental development, or you can separate yourself downwards by preparing poorly.

I frequently tell sport and corporate audiences that two football Hall of Famers highlight the importance of preparation for building confidence. Bill Parcells, a successful NFL coach who transformed four losing teams (NY Giants, NY Jets, New England Patriots, and Dallas Cowboys) into winners, said, "Preparedness is the key to success. The more you prepare beforehand the more relaxed and effective you'll be when it counts."[10] Roger Staubach, an All-Pro NFL quarterback, has said about confidence and success, "The most important thing is preparation. You have to do everything you can to be successful. As an athlete I worked really hard to be ready for the moment. When the moment came, I had paid the price." He went on to say, "It takes a lot of unspectacular preparation to get spectacular results."[11]

Practice the things you have to work on to become a better and more confident golfer. Practice on the tee, practice your fairway shots, practice your short approaches. Practice your putting. Practice to develop "right feeling" and "right focus." With practice you will learn to trust your process so you can play with confidence and impact.

When commenting about Collin Morikawa's remarkable performance in winning the British Open, Rick Sessinghaus, Morikawa's golf and mental coach, said "He has trained like this for a long, long time. Just to see how he stayed calm and focused through all this was amazing. And to see his short game and the mental work he's been putting in on his putting pay off and for him to trust himself down to the stretch." Rick added, "It's just in his nature to be disciplined, goal-oriented, and do what's necessary to get the job done."[12]

It should be noted that swing dynamics can also play a role in "right feeling" and in building or undermining confidence.

I am not a golf instructor or an expert on the biomechanics of the game. However, I work with athletes in many sports. And something I've observed is that athletes with more natural, balanced movement patterns tend to perform/play with more ease, efficiency, and confidence. I believe it's the same in golf. If a golfer's swing dynamics are relatively "natural" (that is, balanced, fluid, and with an economy of movement), then all things being equal, I believe the golfer will perform with less stress and a more confident feeling. If, however, their golf swing appears to be "unnatural" (that is, uncentered and tight, with excessive twisting), even though the golfer may perceive their swing as normal and comfortable, he or she is creating more physical stress and strain, which can lead to feelings of unease that undermine confidence.

Jim Nelford, a player and instructor with a feel for swing dynamics and the mental game, believes that the poor swing dynamics widely being taught can cause tension and anxiety which undermine confidence (see Chapter 2).[13] Similarly, Jordan Spieth also commented that simplifying swing dynamics can improve performance and confidence. Spieth explained that he was suffering from the same complex uptight swing issue that appears in many amateur golf swings. Spieth has been working to simplify his swing feeling. He now swings more around, less up-and-down. After simplifying his swing, Spieth reported feeling more confident in his ability and more trusting in his swing.[14]

Anxiety causes tension and dis-ease. Anxious feelings can reduce performance and erode confidence. Fight or flight is not a good psychophysical basis for golf. Some people feel anxious even when they are relatively well prepared. However, feelings affect thinking. To be a positive, confident thinker you must control your emotions. It's difficult to think positive, confident power thoughts when your heart is racing, breathing is shallow, and a voice somewhere in your consciousness is whispering, "Don't screw up." It's well understood that confidence evolves from improving your skills. That's why golfers work to improve swing mechanics. However, in so doing, they often overthink and complicate the process, which creates feelings of dis-ease and uncertainty. It may be less well appreciated that confidence evolves by learning how to transform the physical feelings of tension and unease into psychophysical feelings of ease and power. A more natural swing — that is, one that is fluid, centered, and balanced — will lead a golfer to feel more comfortable within themselves, which supports consistency and confidence.

"Most golfers prepare for disaster. A good
golfer prepares for success." – Bob Toski

Paul was an enthusiastic club player, a passionate but inconsistent golfer. He sought me out to help him deal with his ups and downs and the frustration it engendered. We did a session of conscious breathing and tension-release but, aside from helping him to relax a little, Paul remarked that he didn't believe that the breathing work would really have much of an impact on his performance. Furthermore, he claimed, "I don't think I tense up much on the course." And he added, "I can relax whenever I want to." So I hooked Paul up to a biofeedback device that measured his heart rate and muscle tension, and asked him to relax. When his biofeedback results indicated Paul was reasonably relaxed, we went out to the practice green. I then asked Paul to putt six balls from 14 feet. I told him if he could make four of the six, I would give him three free sessions and $1000. Paul said, "Bring it on." Paul was again hooked up to a heart rate monitor and a device measuring muscle tension. I mentioned to him that relaxing might help his putting touch. Paul missed his first three putts and, not surprisingly, the two biofeedback modalities indicated Paul was indeed tense. I explained that anxiety and tension do not support consistent confident performance. And, along with working to improve his putting, I suggested it would be advisable to work on his emotional management so he could count on his feelings to be there for him under pressure.

"I think to be 'tough' means you look relaxed.
You have to be tough to win tournaments. But
you don't want to be so tough on yourself."
– Yani Tseng

The conscious breathing and the tension-release process described in Section 2 play a major role in creating feelings of calm, power, control, and balance. They are great ways to recharge and aid in building and maintaining confidence.

Again, I recommend 10 to 15 minutes of conscious breathing not just on competition days but *every* day.

To summarize, here are five keys to building confidence:

1. Know you are a good golfer (or that you are becoming a good golfer), know your strengths, and continuously work to improve.
2. Work to develop right feeling. Define and be comfortable with the specific swing elements that go into making success possible.
3. Work to have right focus. Be positive and clear. Take dead aim.
4. Confidence comes from being strong and in great shape.
5. Love to golf. Love and fear are the core human emotions. Golf is a very mentally and physically challenging sport. *Love the challenge.*

I had a call from a young golfer who was rehabilitating following a postseason shoulder surgery. Her recovery was progressing slowly and she expressed some concerns regarding her readiness and her desire to really do well in her upcoming NCAA season. She said, "I'm just not feeling as confident as I would like to be." I explained that preparation builds confidence and that she simply wasn't physically prepared to perform at her best. The good news was that she had time to heal and that she was enrolled in what appeared to be a very well supervised rehab program. I encouraged her to work on her program and with time she would feel stronger, better prepared, and ultimately more confident.

Love is power. As I said in Chapter 3, the way we are "wired" as human beings, our feelings affect our thinking, and our thinking in turn affects our feelings.

Figure 9.1. As I said in Chapter 3, the way we are "wired" as human beings, our feelings affect our thinking, and our thinking in turn affects our feelings.

Right feeling comes from having the mental skills, the focus, and the emotional control to prepare properly and to deal with the intense feelings generated by the pressure of competition. Being in control requires a special set of psychological skills, skills that can be strengthened with training. Learning to control emotions is a confidence builder that can lead to significant performance increments.

Charles, a young athlete, emailed me the following message after returning home from an important tournament: "Hi, Dr. Miller. I just got back from the tournament. I performed very well though I did have some shaky moments. When these moments occurred, I went back to my breathing, remembered my ABCs, and was fine from then on."

Knowing you have the ability to manage the "shaky" moments builds confidence. Conversely, not having emotional control can lead to inconsistency, disappointing performance experiences, and a lack of confidence.

Design Your Own Confidence-Building Training Program

- Assess and adjust. Think about what elements you have to improve to perform more effectively. Think about what you have to do to really master these elements. What specific skill(s) would improve your confidence?
- Explore how you can improve your emotional control with breathing and the tension-release reflex.
- What self-talk and imagery would help?
- What is the true level of your commitment?
- List three things you can do to build your golf confidence.
- Act on your commitment. Preparation builds confidence. See yourself practicing and improving.

"The most important shot in golf is the next one." – Ben Hogan

I spent several years as a sport psychologist with the Los Angeles Rams in the National Football League. One of the high-pressure jobs in football is field-goal kicker. A kicker's performance can be affected by confidence. At practice, the Rams kicker regularly went through a confidence-building routine. He would start by kicking short field goals, or chip shots, from the 20- or 25-yard-line. After making two or three kicks in a row, he would move to the 30-yard line. With success at each distance, he'd move back farther — to the 35-yard line, 40-yard line, and so on — even varying his angle. As he progressed through this regular practice routine, he strengthened his perception of himself as a competent kicker, and his trust in his ability and his process grew . . . as did his confidence.

Based on what I've observed in every sport, it's clear that confidence flows from preparation and success. Do the physical and mental work necessary to experience success in the elements and steps to your ultimate goal, and your confidence will grow.

DESERVING

A sense of deserving is another expression of a confident, winning attitude. Here, I am not referring to a sense of entitlement. Rather, I'm referring to a confident, aggressive mindset that usually is the product of lots of hard work. Confronted with a challenge, some athletes just go for it. It's as if they feel they deserve it and they're going to take it. Most winners have this quality. They expect to be there, and they don't hesitate to go for it. Others don't feel as confident. It's as though they don't expect success or they need permission to go for it. Sometimes, they think too much.

A sense of deserving is a matter of attitude. It's believing *I deserve to express all of my ability*. It's part of a predator's mindset. There's no holding back. Remember, if you don't believe you deserve it, it's unlikely you're going to make it happen.

Here's a simple three-step process I have found useful in helping athletes strengthen their sense of deserving.

First, sit back and tune in to your breathing rhythm. Allow time for the breath to come all the way in ... and time for it flow all the way out. Relax. Breathe slowly and smoothly. As you do, remind yourself that you deserve your time. What I am referring to is actually *experiencing* the feeling of time, time for the breath to come all the way in ... and time for the breath to go all the way out.

As you begin to experience your breathing rhythm, *acknowledge that you deserve your time*. You don't have to do anything or accomplish anything, you simply deserve the full time for the breath to flow in and out.

Second, understand in the very same way — know and feel — that you deserve to express your athletic ability. Imagine golfing. Visualize yourself performing well, making shots with ease, precision, and confidence. As you do, affirm that *you deserve to express your ability, all your ability*. Know and *feel* that you deserve to express it all.

Third, bring that awareness and sense of deserving to an actual competitive/tournament situation. If you find yourself in a match with a more experienced golfer or someone who may have outperformed you in the past, and if you are feeling less powerful and less confident, then *use* this dis-ease to go deeper into your breathing and acknowledge what you know to be true, "I deserve to express my ability — all my ability." Then become the hunter and bring that sense of deserving into the match.

Know that you deserve to express all your ability. Doing the physical, technical, and mental work builds ability, results, and confidence.

THE YIPS – A LACK OF CONFIDENCE

Most golfers have heard of "the yips." They can be a profound challenge to a golfer's confidence. The term was originally coined by the Scottish golfer Tommy Armour, who described it as a "brain spasm that impairs the short game."[15] Versions of the yips have been known over the years by many names, including "freezing," "the jerks," and "whiskey fingers." The yips are a specific involuntary tensing of certain muscle groups (hands, wrists, arms) that negatively impacts on performance. In golf, it's most frequently seen as a putting problem, but a golfer can also get the yips chipping or even have full-swing yips.

There have been several theories as to what causes the yips. Some say the cause is psychological, some say it's neuromuscular, and some say musculoskeletal. Indeed, I believe there may actually be several different tensing phenomena that are labeled as yips that may be due to different causes. The fact that a golfer can have a good practice stroke or swing and then tense up on the actual shot leads me to believe there is an underlying psychological component at play . . . and confidence is lacking. Further, the fact that performance anxiety in many cases seems to exacerbate the yips also suggests there is a psychological component to the phenomenon — more beta — more tensing and contraction.

Since it's been suggested that there may be different causes for the condition, one might expect a number of different remedies. Some advocate mechanical solutions such as changing the grip, the stance, and the swing to involve using different muscle groups and/or changing the golf club. Certainly, uptight mechanics can contribute to tense play. However, what I have found to be most helpful is mental-skills training. Specifically improving right focus (that is, having a clear sense of direction for the shot to be taken and the belief that "I can") and having right feeling (working with breathing; feeling centered, grounded, and balanced; and experiencing ease and flow in striking the ball), as outlined in Chapters 3 to 9. And remembering to practice with these elements. Practice builds confidence, and that reduces the yips.

Alan was a senior golfer who developed the yips while putting. He first experienced a jerking movement as he was about to make the putt. He commented on something he thought was really strange; his practice stroke seemed okay, but when he got over the ball to stroke it to the hole, "something weird seemed to happen." The more he began to worry about it, the more frequently it happened. When he asked around, people told him it was the yips. Once he believed that he had the yips, it consolidated the problem and became even more of an issue.

The procedure I used with Alan was, first, to explain to him that he didn't have a fixed condition, that, occasionally, anxiety and pressure were causing an interfering, tensing muscular reaction. Then, I had him do some conscious breathing and, in a relaxed state, *imagine* making a smooth putting stroke. When he was comfortable with the breathing and stroke imagery, I had him relax, breathe, and take some actual practice putting strokes with his eyes closed. When he appeared to be comfortable with that, we moved on to his looking at the hole six feet away, closing his eyes, and stroking the ball (actually several balls) toward the hole. After each stroke, I asked Alan, with his eyes still closed, to tell me where the ball went relative to the hole. As Alan began to feel comfortable stroking the ball, he was also developing a better feeling sense of where the ball went. Next, we moved back to eight feet and repeated the process, eyes closed. When Alan became comfortable with the feeling of stroking the ball, accurately sensing where the ball went, and putting the ball closer to the hole, I asked him to go through the same process with his eyes open. With repeated practice, Alan reported feeling more comfortable and confident when putting, and his putting became more accurate. All the while, I reminded Alan that he didn't have a fixed condition, that the task was to regain and then maintain the feel of stroking the ball and the sense of knowing where it would go.

Nobody is perfect. Remember that when you experience a moment of poor performance — *use it*. Use your mistakes to your advantage. Think of what you can do to improve your performance next time. It's always next shot, next hole, next match. Frame your efforts in a positive light. As you do, your performance will improve and your confidence will grow.

TRAINING EXERCISES

1. Continue to do the positive self-talk ("I am a good golfer," etc.). Know your strengths, and do some conscious breathing every day.

2. Do the assess-and-adjust exercise mentioned in the confidence-building section above. Use the self-evaluation form in Chapter 2 to identify aspects of golf that challenge you, where you feel your confidence is limited. Think about what elements you have to improve to perform more effectively. And design your own training program, think about what you have to do to really master these elements.

- What specific skills would improve your confidence?
- What self-talk and imagery would help?
- Discover how you can improve your emotional control with breathing and the release reflex?
- What is the level of your commitment?
- Make a list of what you can do to build your golfing confidence.

3. Build consistency and confidence in your putting. Putting is a critically important part of the game. It's been said, "Drive for show and putt for dough." Well, here are two confidence-building putting exercises mentioned earlier in the chapter. The first exercise builds consistency and confidence. On the putting green, arrange six balls in a three-foot circle around the hole. Make all six putts and repeat the process. It builds trust in your stroke, and that builds confidence. Then, go to six balls from five feet, make all six, and do this twice. Then, go to six balls from 10 feet. Make as many as you can. Do it twice, none finishing outside two feet. Finally, drop six balls from 20 to 30 feet, make as many as you can twice, none finishing outside six feet. As you do this exercise, consistency and confidence will grow.

The second exercise strengthens your *putting feel*. Set up to putt six feet from the hole. Look at the hole, determine line and distance. Then look down at the ball, close your eyes, and putt. With eyes closed, guess how close you came to the hole, how long or short were you. Repeat this process with six balls. Then move back to 10 feet and repeat the process.

CHAPTER TEN

Identity

"I think the game of golf teaches you so much about yourself, like who you really are and what you are made of."
— Stewart Cink

Identity is another ingredient in a winning attitude. Your identity is who you think *and* feel you are — and to a lesser extent, who others perceive you to be. For most of us, our identity evolves with time and experience. Successful athletes have an identity or image of themselves as effective competitors. Your golf identity can affect how you behave and perform. Most important, it's something you can shape and control. As we've said before, you get more of what you think about. If you think you can, you may. If you think you can't, you won't. The way you talk to yourself and visualize yourself performing are two important determinants of your identity or self-image. Your golf identity can give you the energy and confidence that will lift you to excel, or it can act like a weight to draw you down and keep you from reaching your potential.

To succeed, it's essential to believe in yourself and to persevere. After five winless years on the PGA Tour, Tony Finau had this to say after winning the 2021 Northern Trust Championship: "I have an extreme belief in myself. I have to. This game is hard as it is and the guys are so good. If you can't believe you can't beat them, it's an uphill battle. I just continue to believe. I believe in myself. I believe in my team. And I haven't had the win to maybe have the confidence . . . I just have to believe I can go out and beat JT, and I can beat Jon Rahm. I have to believe that. And I did. That's why I sit here today as champion."

And on his perseverance, Tony commented, "I've worked extremely hard, not just on my game but on my body to put myself in these types of situations. Eventually, I knew it was going to happen. It's hard losing. It's hard losing in front of the world. I know I've done it a couple of times this year in playoffs. That made me more hungry. That's what it does if it doesn't discourage you. It makes me more hungry."[1]

> "I have to believe in myself. I know what I
> can do, what I can achieve. . . . I always think
> under par. You have to believe in yourself."
> – Sergio Garcia

Identity is not a static entity. Identity is something that has been formed over time and by experience, and it can be reshaped. You can change your identity by changing your mind. The word "repent" comes from a root word that means to think again. We tend to associate repentance with a particular kind of mind change, with making a commitment to stop sinning. Well, when you think negative things about yourself and the way you perform, you create a loser's identity, and that is a form of sinning. It's limiting, and it's a signal that it's time to re-think. Change your mind. Having a winning golf mindset means creating a positive self-image. Remember, you're the boss, and attitude is a matter of choice.

In Chapter 5, three positive focusing exercises were presented:

1. Think, "I'm a good golfer," and know your strength.
2. Visualize the actions you do when you are performing at your best.
3. Use affirmations or power statements to define and strengthen your identity.

As I said before, your affirmations should represent who you are and what you aspire to be.

CREATE AN IDENTITY STATEMENT

Write a statement of who you are, and who you could be at your best. Affirm all your strengths and highlight your potential. If there is a desired quality that you haven't yet manifested, incorporate it into your identity statement. If you are truly uncomfortable saying to yourself, "I am a good golfer," then say, "I am becoming a good golfer."

Read this statement to yourself frequently and repeat it often. Let it become you. When you have a good performance acknowledge it, *use it*. Say to yourself, "That's who I am." Reinforce your positive sense of self, your identity as a good golfer.

When you perform poorly, don't latch on to that disappointing perception and keep rerunning it as to who you are. Don't let a bad start or a bad shot become a bad competition. Again, *use it*. Release the negative — take a breath, and say to yourself, "That's not me." Then, imagine and feel yourself performing well. Remember, to improve your performance identity (and increase your confidence), think about and visualize you performing at your best, then work toward making it a reality.

Here's an interesting identity anecdote from another sport: While working with a group of world-class cyclists prior to the Seoul Olympics, I talked to them about Greg LeMond. LeMond was the first North

American to win the grueling Tour de France bicycle race. Shortly after winning the Tour in 1986, he was accidentally shot while hunting with his brother-in-law in California. He had over 35 shotgun pellets in his body and sustained serious wounds to his lungs, intestines, liver, and his one functioning kidney. There was significant blood loss and several broken ribs. There were pellets left in his body, some in the lining of his heart and his liver. LeMond ended up losing 20 percent of his body weight. A slow, painful recovery followed. A year later, LeMond was finally able to return to racing. At one of his first races back, it was said LeMond looked terrible, pale and thin, not in top form; however, when the breakaway group separated itself from the pack, there was LeMond in the break with them.

I remember asking the riders present, "How was it possible that LeMond, who had almost died a few months before and was clearly not in top form, could be in the breakaway group?" Gervais Rioux, one of the racers, replied, "Because that's where he thought he belonged."[2] Indeed, at the front of the pack is where LeMond believed he belonged.

Remarkably, Greg LeMond went on to win two more Tour de France competitions, in 1989 and 1990. Our identity, our sense of self can have a profound effect on how we perform and handle life's challenges.

For too many athletes, their sense of well-being is determined by how they perform. If they do well, they feel good about themselves. If they perform poorly, they feel terrible, even worthless. It's normal for people who are highly motivated and who work very hard to achieve certain performance goals to be disappointed with poor performance. However, it's important to stay positively focused on your commitment. Remember and affirm that you are on a positive track and that nothing can take you off that track. Whenever you have a good workout, practice, or match, acknowledge yourself. Rerun your highlight reel, either on video or with mental rehearsal imagery. Work at continuously improving your golfing process. And repeat those positive self-statements and power thoughts.

BUILDING PRIDE

Most golfers have heard the word, and many coaches often use it to rally their athletes. I asked a 15-year-old athlete, "What does pride mean to you?" Without a moment's hesitation, she replied, "It's feeling good about what I do."

Pride is a composite of many qualities of a winning attitude. It's related to commitment, confidence, identity, and self-esteem. Pride is having a positive sense of who you are, how you choose to represent yourself, and what you have done. Performing well requires preparation, so take pride in consistently preparing to be at your best. Take pride in preparing physically, technically, and mentally, and in your commitment to being the best you can be.

> "Great champions have an enormous sense of pride. The people who excel are those who are driven to show the world and prove to themselves just how good they are."
> – Nancy Lopez

Five Steps to Building Pride

1. Relax and breathe. Relaxed conscious breathing can help you to improve your sense of self and the quality of your thoughts and images.

2. Imagine and create the feelings you have when you are golfing to the best of your ability. Visualize yourself making all the

shots (off the tee, on fairways, approaching the green, and putting). Acknowledge these positive images. Say, "That's who am." Take on that identity of you at your best.

3. Make the commitment to be the best you can be. Affirm you are willing to do whatever it takes to be the golfer you aspire to be. Do the work to make it happen — in the gym, on the range, on the golf course. Combine that with mental training. Be consistent. Work at it every day. Commit to giving a hundred percent every training session and every match.

When Rick Sessinghaus was asked about his first impression of Collin Morikawa — he began coaching him at eight years old — he replied, "He was amazing from an early age, very coachable, very curious, very intelligent . . . always asking good questions. You don't normally get that from an eight-, nine-, 10-year-old. With that, it's easy as a coach to get excited because someone wants to learn. He always wanted to learn and he never looked at failure as a bad thing, just something he could learn from. So, it was great seeing a young player who just wanted to embrace getting better and having the discipline to do it."[3]

Being interviewed after winning the 2020 Masters, Dustin Johnson was uncharacteristically emotional. When asked about it, he replied, "It's a dream come true. As a kid, I always dreamed about being a Masters champion. It means so much to me, to my family. . . . They know it's something I've always been dreaming about and it's why I work so hard. Yeah, I put in a lot of work off the golf course, on the golf course, and you know I think it's just something you do, something you push yourself for. . . . That's why I work so hard. It's to be in this position. And you know, to finally have the dream come true. I think that's why you see all that emotion."[4]

4. Evaluate your progress. Assess and adjust. Find something positive to acknowledge, even if it's just your dedication and work ethic. Find an area of your game that needs more attention and work to improve it. Commit to consistently working to strengthen what you are good at and to improve the things in your game that can be better.

5. Walk your talk. Be a model of commitment and determination. As you put your heart and soul into being the best golfer you can be, slowly but surely your sense of pride in who you are, what you are trying to accomplish, and what you are able to do will grow day by day.

LOVE

Last but not least, love the sport. I encourage you to think about love. See how it can benefit your game. Love is an antidote to fear. And fear is the most limiting program that golfers run on their mental computers. Fear has many faces — fear of failure, fear of embarrassment, fear of not meeting expectations, fear of letting others down, fear of losing control, fear of getting hurt, fear of the unknown, and even fear of success. Fear causes tension. Fear cuts down breathing, reduces energy flow, and ultimately limits performance.

At the beginning of the book, I quoted Sam Snead, who is known to have said, "Of all the hazards, fear is the worst."[5]

Love is more powerful than fear. Love is expansive. It opens us to new possibilities. Love and creative thought are two of the most powerful forces available to us as human beings. When we combine love with talent and training, remarkable things are possible. Interesting? Perhaps. But does it relate to golf? It absolutely does! Golf is a very exacting, challenging sport. It's both physically and mentally challenging. Love the challenge. Love to play golf. Love is a winning golf psychology *core concept*. Good things flow from that.

> "I love to play golf and that's my arena.
> And you can characterize it and describe it
> however you want, but I have a love and a
> passion for getting the ball in the hole and
> beating those guys." – Tiger Woods

Phil Mickelson has been winning on the PGA Tour for 30 years, with talent, passion, and hard work. Still, at the age of 50 and with 44 PGA Tour victories behind him, his love of the game and his love to compete seemingly haven't diminished. Phil described why his competitive golfing passion remains intense: "I find myself just internally motivated because of my love to compete and my love to try to bring out the best in me. It's the ability to play and compete against the best in the world that gets me in the gym every morning at 6 or 7, that gets me on the range working on my game, on the putting green working on my putting."[6] At any age, love supports the work and nurtures the talent to make things happen.

Passion and hard work deliver. Several months after making the above comments, and at the age of 50, Phil Mickelson won the PGA Championship in Kiawah Island, South Carolina, and further distinguished himself by being the oldest golfer to win a PGA Major.

Feel the Love

Recall some of the golf imagery we discussed earlier. Again, love the challenge. Love being out there on the edge. Love pushing the envelope. Love to score and enjoy being around athletes who love the sport.

Love is power. Think loving thoughts about yourself. I often coach my clients that *self-love is allowing yourself to be great.* And the easiest ways to love yourself are by taking a breath and by saying positive things to yourself.

Thinking loving thoughts about golf can make it easier to handle golf's more challenging moments. Your passion for the sport can help you tap a limitless power source. Fear can sometimes stimulate action; it can kick-start you to get going. But the greatest performances come when people go beyond fear and move into the love zone. Again, love to drive off the tee, love to hit long and straight on the fairways, love to pitch and approach with accuracy, love to putt with touch. Love the challenge, love to compete, love pushing yourself into the unknown, love to win. Love this wonderful sport.

An elderly friend of mine named Bill Walker is a remarkable athlete. Bill is a *very* keen golfer who has been golfing for 80 years. When he retired from teaching in 1988, Bill rode his motorcycle to every state in the continental USA (including Alaska) to play golf. I asked him if he was the first person to ride a motorcycle to every state in the USA to play golf, and he replied, "I think I'm the only person to have done it." Bill currently plays golf four to five days a week and is quite capable of shooting his age (90).

When I asked Bill what advice he has for golfers, he said, "*The most important thing is to love the game . . . really enjoy it.* Golf is a very demanding and exacting sport, and if you don't really enjoy playing, then it's easy to be frustrated by a couple of poor shots. Love insulates us from any real emotional upsets on errant shots or a bad bounce." Bill recalled seeing plenty of emotional outbursts on the links over the years, including swearing and tossing clubs aside. Bill described seeing one enraged golfer wrap his club around a tree and another frustrated golfer throw his golf club bag into a pond and storm off to his car, only to realize when he got to his car that his car keys were in the golf bag.

Bill said, "If you truly love playing golf, and you aren't out there to prove something to yourself, or to others, well then, I just don't think you get that upset."[7]

While playing a round of golf with Bill a couple of years ago, I was struggling with an old putter that I had in my bag. When I complained about the club, Bill said, "Let's just switch clubs," and handed me his fine putter. He then proceeded to putt very effectively with my old putter while I continued to struggle with his. Often it's not the club but the golfer's mindset that needs to be changed. Bill's ability to embrace the game as well as his talent enabled him to perform very effectively. Loving the challenge helps you to excel; seeing the challenge as a struggle can do just the opposite.

A NEW IDENTITY

Robert was a very good collegiate golfer. He struggled after turning pro. We met when Robert was preparing for a second go on one of the lesser pro tours. Robert was a bright, thoughtful golfer, who was very focused on results and also on the significant financial cost of being on tour. To reduce his anxiety and excessive result-focus we worked with right focus and right feeling, particularly positive self-talk, visualization, conscious breathing, and the release reflex. I reminded Robert that ultimate performance is always a combination of pleasure and precision. And I encouraged him to reflect on his love of golf to bring more enjoyment to this game. Thereafter, Robert reported there was some improvement in his performance.

Then, a couple of months later, Robert called while at a tournament in the Midwest. He described experiencing a real feeling of panic on the golf course, something he had never felt before. After some discussion and a suggestion he do some conscious breathing, I related to Robert what I thought was going on. I told him I thought it was his excessive focus on the end result, the frustration with his lack of progress on the tour, worries about his financial situation, and the unsettling sense that he might not "make it" and achieve his goal of being a PGA Tour player — all these thoughts coming together in his mind created panic.

I then suggested Robert experience a shift in identity. I told him to create a new golfer's identity — specifically, to select a new name and adopt the persona of a talented golfer: a wealthy and carefree player who loves to golf, who hits the ball long and straight, has a good approach game (as Robert does), and who putts with confidence.

Robert agreed to give it a try. To which, I said, "Don't try, but as Nike says, *'Just do it.'*" Robert texted me the next day that the name of his new golf persona was Jesse — "like Jesse James" — and confirmed that Jesse was a confident, carefree, talented player who had money and who loved to golf.

Jesse played well . . . and so did Robert.

Competitive golf is like a mirror. In keeping with Stewart Cink's quote at the beginning of the chapter: competitive golf provides an opportunity to learn and grow and to discover what you have to work on to become a more complete athlete . . . and person.

Golf is a very mentally and physically challenging sport. Love the sport and love the challenge it presents.

TRAINING EXERCISES

1. Take a look at your identity and confidence. Think of your strengths as a golfer and write them down. Consider the elements that make you effective. Note what you have to do to maintain these strengths. Develop a practice program that will maintain your competence at the things you are good at. As you work on your program, use positive self-talk, power words, and imagery. Strengthen your identity as a consistently good golfer.

Think of an area you must improve as a golfer and write it down. Consider the elements necessary for you to be more competent in this area. List the things you could do to improve. Develop a training schedule with steps and stages to improve in this area. As you work on your program, use positive self-talk, power words, and positive imagery. Bolster your identity as someone who is a good golfer.

2. Review and edit your identity statement. Repeat it to yourself at least once a day. Make it a regular part of your training program and preparation.

3. Love the sport. Grow your passion for golf. Start to use love as a power word in your training. Love is one of the most powerful forces you can have working for you. Love to play. Love to practice. Love to compete. Love a challenge. Love to dominate. Love yourself. Love the situation you're in.

    Continue working with all your power words and affirmations. Keep using them. Repetition builds strength. If a couple of words or statements don't feel right to you, let them go. Always be looking for new words. Add a new word that gives you an edge and drop a word that you're not using or that no longer has power for you.

CHAPTER ELEVEN

Balance and Lifestyle

"The proper score for a businessman golfer is 90.
If he's better than that, he's neglecting his business.
If he's worse, he's neglecting his golf." – Golf saying

Balance is about harmony. Imbalance creates stress. That's true of a golf swing, and it's true about life. Most high-performance athletes can appreciate the importance of balance and lifestyle, both in supporting their well-being and in their quest for success. By lifestyle I simply mean the way we live day to day. That includes energy and time management, diet, exercise, rest and recreation, relationships, and attitude. As with any group, there are vast individual differences in lifestyle among golfers. The following are some general ideas that apply to most athletes.

ENERGY AND TIME MANAGEMENT

In order to be a healthy and consistently successful performer, it's key to manage one's time and energy effectively. One golfer who really impressed me with her ability to manage her energy well was Nancy Lopez. Nancy was a remarkable golfer. While consulting with her at the Dinah Shore Nabisco Classic in Palm Springs, I experienced her remarkable capacity to manage her time and energy. On the day we were to meet, I arrived at the course early, around 8 a.m., and watched Nancy warm up before her morning tee off. I walked the course watching her play an effective round of golf. After her round and a brief break, she had lunch with a family member. After lunch, she practiced her short game and participated in a photo shoot for a book she was working on. Then we connected and went to the condo she had rented with her family. Her young daughters were excited to see her, and she spent some time with them before we sat down and spent an hour and a half reviewing techniques for maintaining right focus and right feeling. When I left, it was late afternoon. I felt I had spent a relatively full day, but Nancy was scheduled for more. She was to attend a banquet that evening. The next day, she was again totally present and competing at a superior LPGA level.

Observing and consulting with this remarkable athlete for a day, I was impressed not only with her extraordinary talent and her engaging personality but also with her ability to manage her time and energy so effectively. Years later, I mentioned to Nancy how impressed I was with the *calm and focus* with which she handled everything. I added that I believed the ability to handle the diversity of things involved with being a competitive pro golfer was a factor in being a successful Tour player. Nancy replied, "You have to be organized. Really. And fortunately, I'm that kind of person. I can organize and plan. I was never a spur-of-the-moment person. I had to plan things, and the calm in me was there when I knew everything was settled and was taken care of."[1]

To stay healthy and be consistently successful in the competitive world of golf (and in life), it helps to balance action with ease, and take time to recharge. Learning to bring ease to the moment (with right feeling and right focus) will enable you to keep stress levels low and help you (with planning and discipline) to manage your time and energy effectively.

Brooke Henderson, a PGA winner who loves the game, commented, "I like to play golf a lot and I considered taking a week off, but then I thought, like what am I going to do? I'm just going to go home and practice. I might as well just go and play . . . and conserve energy where I am . . . and focus on the things I need to do."

On another occasion, Brooke commented on being tired and expecting herself to play better than she did, "I just wasn't able to perform at the same level," said Henderson. "I definitely learned from it and how important proper rest is before a major."[2]

DIET

Now, let's look at diet. When I worked in the NFL with the Los Angeles Rams, I remember cringing at the fast-food dietary habits a few players exhibited, including having Cokes and doughnuts for breakfast. The players' parking lot was filled with high-priced luxury cars and high-performance sports cars, so I said to some players, "You wouldn't put junk fuel in your car and expect it to perform well. Why do you put it in a high-performance energy system like your own body?"

Individual athletes differ markedly in terms of body type, goals, metabolism, personality, experience, and preferences. Some younger athletes feel they can eat anything (and they often do) without noticing it affecting them. More serious and mature athletes tend to have developed an appreciation of how the foods they eat affect performance.

As a golfer you probably want foods that will give you energy, clarity, strength, and endurance. Many nutritional experts recommend a diet rich in complex carbohydrates, high in fiber, low in fat, with a moderate amounts of quality protein. Hydrating, drinking plenty of fluids, is essential. Increasingly, serious athletes are going to broad spectrum supplements (e.g., multivitamins, zinc, creatine, etc.) and protein drinks to complement a healthy diet. And most experts suggest eliminating or cutting way back on processed and sugary foods.

For pre-competition meals, eat something that is easy to digest. Experiment intelligently. Find out what works for you. Take stock of the foods you are used to eating and try to recall what has nurtured good performances in the past. One way to keep track of how your diet affects how you perform is to record what you eat in a performance journal (if you keep one). It's important that you do what works for you.

When I asked one of my successful golf clients what changes he made with nutrition that benefited his performance, he replied, "If I eat something before a match and I don't feel well and play poorly, I won't eat that again."

Diet is a personal matter. Again, it's what works for you. Rory McIlroy has shared some thoughts on following a diet on golf days that works for him: "On the course I sometimes eat a little sandwich or a slow-release energy bar. One on the front nine and one on the back nine. You are out there for five hours so you have to keep eating. You are going to burn at least 1000 calories. I try to take in 400–600 calories during a round and drink water." (It's important to stay well hydrated especially when playing in warm, sunny conditions.) Rory added, "If I'm playing in the morning, I'll get some carbs early: porridge with chopped banana. If I'm playing in the afternoon, I'll start with less carbs and have some eggs and fruit for breakfast, then a light lunch 90 minutes before I play so I don't feel sluggish or full."[3]

Tiger Woods confesses to having a healthy appetite. When asked about his diet, he said, "If I'm at home, then I eat five to seven meals in a day. I'm always hungry. I struggle with keeping my weight up so if I don't eat enough then I typically lose weight very quickly." He commented that he takes his diet very seriously: "When it comes to eating right, I'm pretty easy to please. I stick to lean meats and seafood, lots of fruits and vegetables, and no junk food. My typical breakfast is an egg-white omelette with vegetables. Lunch and dinner is usually grilled chicken or fish with salad and vegetables. Protein ranks high in my diet because it helps build muscle tissue. I also take daily supplements for bone protection and nutritional support."

Woods recently tweeted that his favorite thing to eat on the course is a peanut butter and banana sandwich and almonds. Frequent spectators have also seen Woods munch on a piece of fruit between holes, specifically apples and bananas.[4]

Jim Furyk, the 2003 U.S. Open champion and the only repeat member of our PGA Tour sub-60 club, maintains a healthy diet filled with fruits, vegetables, and plenty of vitamin D and calcium to keep his bones strong. On the course, he likes to keep energy bars on hand to sustain him. Reports are that Furyk is particularly fond of Lärabars.[5]

Acclaimed golfer Phil Mickelson initially adopted a vegetarian diet in 2010 after being diagnosed with psoriatic arthritis, but after five months he went back to eating meat. Mickelson still maintains a vegetable-heavy diet but supplements with lean meats and proteins. He has been spotted eating fruit and staying hydrated on the course.[6]

Alternatively, Bryson DeChambeau has found that a high protein diet works for him. He said, "I've tried the keto diet and all these things, but what I've found is that as long as I'm keeping a 2:1 ratio of carbs to protein, that works for me." DeChambeau maintains his muscle mass with several hearty meals and up to seven protein shakes a day. Breakfast is usually four eggs, five pieces of bacon, toast, and two protein shakes. After breakfast, he hits the golf course for practice. During that time, he eats several Macro bars, a peanut butter and jelly sandwich, and three protein shakes. His post-golf snack includes yet another protein shake. Dinner is generally steak, potatoes, and two more protein shakes. DeChambeau does not count calories. However, he estimates eating between 3000 and 3500 calories per day.[7]

There is no one diet that is right for everyone. Discover what works best for you. Again, a good way to start to manage your golf nutrition intelligently is to keep a record of what you eat for a couple of weeks.

Don't change anything. Be completely honest. Write down everything. Often, our daily eating patterns aren't what we think they are. Hydrating is important. You might think that you're drinking plenty of water, but when you write it down you may find that you're drinking far less than you thought you were. Once you see your actual dietary patterns, make appropriate adjustments and observe how that affects the quality of your training and competition.

EXERCISE

Most golfers get plenty of exercise. Increasingly, competitive golfers are working out and building strength and fitness all year long. Physical training is a great way to prove the old saying that what you put in (to your training and practice) is what you get out (in performance, power, endurance, focus, and precision). Being in good shape improves both physical and mental performance. Sergio Garcia has said, "Concentrating for four hours will wear you out."[8] One solution is to be fit.

A client of mine, named Coleman, loved to golf. Even in his late 70s he preferred to walk the course and play without a cart. However, recently he began to comment on the effects of aging and the importance of exercise. He said, "I've been noticing when I have fatigue, I just don't concentrate as well" — an observation that applies to many younger golfers as well. Coleman continued, "If I want to play like I know I still can, then I'm going to have to work out more than I do."[9]

> "Going to the gym is great for your body but
> it's also great for your mind." – Rory McIlroy

No question, fitness is vital to consistent high-level performance. Moe Norman, a remarkable and eccentric professional and a member of Canada's Golf Hall of Fame, had this to say about working out. "I don't understand why anyone would go to the gym to get in shape to play golf. If you hit 600 balls a day, walk a lot, and watch your diet, you'll get in shape. I don't think Sam Snead ever went to the gym, and nobody today is in better shape than he was. Hitting balls is the best workout there is."[10]

Work hard. You are not a machine. Employ balance. Add diversity to your athletic activity. Overtraining can ultimately limit enthusiasm and athleticism. Take time off. Find ways to cross-train. Whenever you can, balance activity and rest. And remember what I said earlier: fitness and strength build confidence and a positive mindset.

R&R

As I said, balance is a key to consistent development. Striking a balance between work and rest is essential. Rest is vital to good performance, and it should be quality rest. You can improve the quality of your rest by developing the conscious breathing and relaxation presented in Chapters 3 and 4. Learn to incorporate breathing/relaxation breaks during your day. Meditation is another excellent restful and restorative balancing technique. Mindfulness meditation is about monitoring the thoughts going through your head, and can therefore improve your ability to recognize when you are experiencing anxious, negative thoughts and feelings. There are some excellent meditation apps available today. Jon Kabat-Zinn, a well-known health and meditation teacher, has said, "One reason I practice meditation is to maintain my own balance and clarity of mind in the face of such huge challenges, and to be able to stay more or less on course through all the weather changes that I encounter day in and day out on this journey."[11]

Getting enough sleep is extremely important. Sleep is the ultimate quality recharge time. Just as you schedule time for training, you need to make sure you get sufficient rest and your sleep needs are met.

Recreation means "re-creation." The most popular "recreational" activity in North America is watching TV, but TV is neither renewing nor recharging. Balance activity with rest, routine with spontaneity, and do things that are fun. Many distractions surround the sport, especially at the higher levels. Make time to rest and recharge free of distraction and energy-draining activities. Develop a good R&R program.

RELATIONSHIPS

We are social animals. The relationships you have with others are an important part of your life. Committed and career athletes, who invest a great deal of their energy in their sport, usually rely on and benefit from nurturing, supportive family and friends, and a team of sport professionals. Bubba Watson has said, "I have a good team around me. I have people I trust around me. If I go the wrong way, they will yell at me. Just as they have in the past."[12]

Lydia Ko on relationships: "I had so much support from my family, no matter if I shoot 81 or 61 they don't love me more or less. Sean [Foley] has been helpful when he says even if you win it doesn't make you a better person. Yes, it's going to make me a little happier at that moment but it doesn't change anything else. He's helped me to clear up questions in my mind and really embrace myself for who I am and accept and be grateful for everything."

She added, "I have a very supportive family, team, and friends that have kind of built the confidence in me. It makes me grateful that I have loving people around me that are supporting me no matter what."[13]

It is a team effort. After winning the LPGA Championship in 2021, Nelly Korda praised her caddie. "Honestly, I was pretty uneasy all day. I was not hitting it good. I was not hitting enough greens. I was not hitting it great off the tee. I just kept it together. . . . My caddie was definitely a big part of why I'm here today holding up the trophy. He's kept me calm and he's someone I can vent on. And he said, 'If you need to snap on someone, you can snap on me.' Sometimes it's great to get it out. And Jason [McDede] is such a great team player and I owe a lot of my success to him."[14]

Similarly, after winning the 2019 Taiwan Swinging Skirts, Korda was quoted as acknowledging her caddie's support, "I wouldn't be where I am without Jason, and he made sure that he kept me in the game."[15]

If you are fortunate enough to have a support team and/or relationship(s) with people who support you and are understanding of your needs, your moods, and your anxieties during the golf season, remember that the off-season is payback time, and that means it's your turn to spend time and energy nurturing and supporting *them*. Create and nurture the supportive relationships that help you relax, prepare, and perform well. Appreciate what others do for you. Acknowledge their love and support. And reciprocate when you can.

ATTITUDE

Attitude is also very much a part of a healthy, high-performance lifestyle. As we said at the start of this section, attitude is a matter of choice, and it's a key component of a healthy lifestyle. Choose to be positive and happy.

> "Keep your sense of humor. There is enough
> stress in the rest of your life to not let bad
> shots ruin a game you're supposed to enjoy."
> – Amy Alcott

There are two elements of attitude I would like to remind you to bring to your daily life: *gratitude* and *love*.

GRATITUDE

By gratitude, I mean appreciating what you have and not dwelling on what's missing. Many athletes know people who are far less fortunate than they are. Don't sweat the small stuff. Every day, be grateful for your health and energy and the opportunity to enjoy performing in a sport you love. A simple powerful meditative exercise I do and recommend to strengthen your sense of gratitude is, every day remind yourself of three things that you are truly grateful for.

In an interview, Max Homa remarked, "I just tell myself positive affirmations especially when I wake up, when I'm nervous on certain tee shots, when I feel I might be getting antsy. I just say three things I'm grateful for. It kind of calms me down. I feel like a lot of people are going through a lot harder stuff than me standing up on 18. I'm grateful for that."

When the interviewer asked, "How many times did you do that today?"

Homa replied, "Probably, 6 or 7 times today. I just do it a lot. It's a good way to just stay happy. Golf is my life but I don't want it to consume me. I want to win. I want to be the best player in the world at some point, one day. I want to be the best me I can be. And all that kind of comes with being a happy dude. So, I'm just trying to be a happy dude."[16]

LOVE

> "I love it. . . . I love playing golf and competing against these guys. These are the best moments ever, because the nerves push you to be a better person."[17] – Collin Morikawa

Love also means accepting and respecting people and opportunity in your life. Be kind and positive with those you work with and those who support you. And live the golden rule: Do unto others as you would have them do unto you.

I wish you good health and much golf enjoyment and success. Now, get to work.

TRAINING EXERCISES

1. Examine your eating habits. For 10 days, write down everything you eat and drink. Be honest. Then review your record and find ways you can improve your eating habits to be a healthier and better golfer.

2. For relaxation and balance, do the breath work every day. Explore possible meditation apps (e.g., Headspace, Calm, Waking Up).

3. Respect and acknowledge the people who support you.

4. Every day, remind yourself of three things for which you are truly grateful.

CHAPTER TWELVE

Individual Differences

The first eleven chapters of the book outlined some basic mental training principles and skills for improving your golf performance. Although these principles and techniques apply to almost everyone, people are different. I thought it might be of interest to discuss a few of the ways that golfers differ from each other and suggest how these differences may affect preparation, dealing with pressure, and competitive performance.

Golfers differ in many ways. They differ in physical attributes such as size, strength, and skill level; they also differ psychologically, in attitude, experience, intelligence, and personality. As a golfer, it is beneficial to understand your psychological makeup so that you are able to create the optimal mental state to excel. (And, as a coach, it is important to know your own personality style as well as the mental makeup of your golf clients in order to more effectively instruct and empower them to be at their best.)

Consider pressure — most people perform at their best by staying relatively calm under pressure. However, there are individuals who seem to thrive under intense pressure and seek out challenging situations to pump themselves up. A key to facilitating performance is to discover what works best for you. Below, three exceptional golfers report feeling and responding to pressure differently.

Jack Nicklaus: "Pressure creates tension and, when you are tense, you want to get the task over as fast as possible. The more you hurry in golf, the worse you probably will play, which leads to heavier pressure and even greater tension. To avoid this vicious circle, I'll take a few deep breaths and quickly review why I'm doing what I'm doing."[1]

Dustin Johnson: "I have always been a fast player. . . . There's only two things that can happen, you hit a good shot or a bad shot, so why waste time doing it?"[2]

Nancy Lopez: "The pressure makes me more intent on each shot. Pressure on the last few holes makes me play better."[3]

Personality differences exist among golfers. What's relevant is how these personality differences may affect preparation and performance. There are a number of personality measures differentiating people. We will look at just two psychological tests — the Myers Briggs Type Indicator (MBTI) and the Test of Attentional and Interpersonal Style (TAIS) — that highlight some of these differences.

THE MYERS BRIGGS TYPE INDICATOR (MBTI)

The MBTI differentiates people on four dimensions: introversion-extroversion, thinking-feeling, detailers-generalizers, routine-spontaneity. We'll explore three of these dimensions.

Introverts and Extroverts

Are you an introvert or an extrovert? One of the more differentiating features of personality that accounts for varying styles and ability to handle pressure is *introversion* and *extroversion*. People commonly use the term "introvert" to refer to someone who is quiet, reserved, and focused within, and "extrovert" to refer to someone who is outgoing or stimulus-seeking.

In Chapter 3, I pointed out a direct relationship between emotional intensity and performance. With either too much or too little emotional intensity, performance is less than optimal. This relationship is depicted in figure 12.1 (similar to figure 3.1).

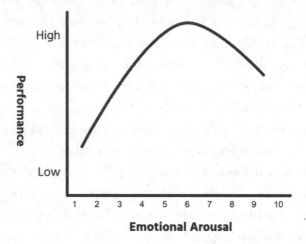

Figure 12.1. The relationship between performance and emotional arousal.

When I ask my clients, "On a scale of 1 to 10, at what number of emotional arousal or intensity do you think you would perform at your best?" most golfers seem to have a reasonably good idea as to what number best represents their optimal performance point. The relationship between emotional arousal and performance can be affected by a personality factor like introversion-extroversion. In general, introverts tend to be more arousal sensitive and get overwhelmed more readily than extroverts. In contrast, extroverts tend to be more stimulus-seeking and may require a higher level of arousal to be at their best. This relationship is depicted in figure 12.2.

In terms of pre-match preparation, this can mean that introverts may perform better if they have a clearly defined pre-match routine to help them manage their emotions and feel calm. This reduces unnecessary last-minute surprises, confusion, and rushing, all of which can be anxiety producing and counterproductive. Introverts appreciate order. They prefer things to occur as scheduled, to have ample time to warm up, to know their equipment is as it should be, and that they are well prepared.

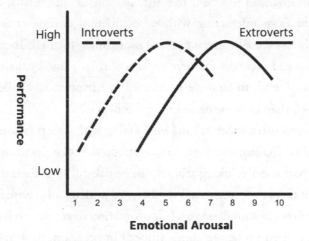

Figure 12.2. How the relationship between performance and emotional arousal is affected by introversion and extroversion.

A possible downside, however, is that introverts sometimes become pre-occupied with the minor details and rituals of preparation and can upset themselves with small deviations in their pre-competition routine. To allay any potential anxiety, introverts can benefit from being relaxed and reassured that they are prepared, everything is as it should be, and that they can deal with any minor alteration in routine or schedule that may present itself. A pre-competition conscious breathing session, positive self-talk, and mental rehearsal are all useful mental skills for the more introverted golfer.

Extroverts appreciate stimulation, interaction, and even a challenge to get into their optimal arousal zone. In the extreme, they may have difficulty organizing well in advance and often wait until the last minute to get going. This can lead to some last-minute confusion regarding warming up and scheduling their time. It's advisable to encourage extroverts to structure a pre-match preparation routine that helps them do what's necessary to get themselves ready to play.

Another distinction between introverts and extroverts is that the latter tend to be more social and outgoing. In getting up for competition, the extrovert is more apt to get energy from the competitive confrontation ahead — from the anticipation of "me, or us, against them," and from interacting with or competing against others. The introvert is less socially interactive and more inner-focused. They prefer to warm up and mentally rehearse aspects of their game by themselves. The introvert tends to be more motivated by the personal challenge to execute well than by wanting to impress others.

Extroverts often enjoy talking and joking with others before competition, even challenging them. Introverts, on the other hand, are more apt to prepare quietly; joking around can be a disturbing distraction for them right before competition. I've observed athletes who were aggressive extroverts use stimulation and confrontation to get themselves (and teammates) fired up before competition. On occasion, they may even challenge their teammates to "show up." For some athletes, a direct in-your-face challenge can spark them to perform well. For others, it has exactly the opposite effect.

Bubba was an introverted collegiate golfer on an NCAA team I worked with. The word was that Bubba played his best golf early in the morning when no one was around, playing by himself and at his own pace. Playing in competition when the pace was quicker and other golfers sometimes made comments negatively affected Bubba's game. To help Bubba, first we did some emotional management using conscious breathing and release-reflex training to give him more emotional control. We also worked with some positive self-talk which involved Bubba acknowledging his strength as a golfer and incorporating the thought "I can handle it" to go along with the release reflex. Thereafter, we paired Bubba for practice rounds with teammates who were specifically instructed to talk with him and at him, to encourage him to play a little quicker, and to generally try to get him off his game. As Bubba came to tolerate them, the assigned agitators' repertoire progressed from being slightly annoying to more so.

Bubba, of course, remained an introvert, but with training and practice his ability to tune out distraction improved as did his tournament play. We knew we had achieved a significant degree of success when

Bubba was paired for a NCAA tournament round with an extroverted golfer named Todd. As they were loosening up near the first tee, Todd whispered to Bubba, "Today, I'm going to kick your ass." Recalling the experience Bubba said, "It surprised me, but I took a breath and reminded myself, 'I'm a good golfer. I can handle this nonsense.'" Bubba went on to play a solid round.[4]

Another example of how introverts and extroverts prepare and react differently occurred while I was working as a sport psychologist with the NHL's Los Angeles Kings. I made a generic pregame warm-up recording for all the players. It contained the "right feeling, right focus" formula outlined in Chapters 3 to 6, with an emphasis on being calm and visualizing oneself performing well. About two weeks after the recordings went out, Sean, one of the players, an extrovert, asked to meet to me. When we met, he said, "Thanks a lot for the recording, Dr. Miller. I've listened to it a few times, and I've got to be honest with you. . . . Before a game, I play much better if someone yells at me and really gives me shit. That's what helps me to get going."[5] Although I didn't give him exactly what he asked for, I did make another recording for him that combined positive, high-performance imagery with aggressive, challenging, confrontational comments.

Most people have some idea where they fit on the introversion-extroversion continuum. If you are interested in more definitive and scientific feedback on where you are on this continuum, I'd recommend taking the Myers Briggs Type Indicator test. Another MBTI dimension contrasts the more analytic and task-oriented individual with the more feeling- and people-oriented person.

Thinkers and Feelers

Another personality style difference between golfers is that some are more thinking, analytical, and task-oriented while others are more feeling and people-oriented. This style difference is a matter of perspective. Analytic, task-oriented golfers are primarily concerned with the specific elements of the task at hand. They may hyper-analyze swing mechanics, overthink the ball-striking process, and continually assess and reassess how they are performing in the match. They are more responsive to coaching input that is specific, mechanical, and task-related. And they respond best to being acknowledged for a specific competency. Because of their task focus, at times these players may appear to be less emotional and less sensitive and/or indifferent to the feelings of others.

Feeling-oriented players are more socially conscious. They are concerned with how they feel and how others see and feel about them. They tend to play with emotion and respond to a pat on the back. They appreciate people acknowledging them for who they are (e.g., "You're a very good player"). They can get upset if they feel they are being rated below another team member or opponent. Danny, one of my clients expressed his extroverted-feeling style nicely when he said, "I think golfing prowess is so extraordinarily admired by others that the extrovert in me wants to show how worthy I am to be considered special."

Coaches would do best to be aware of these differences in perceptual style. They should recognize that some golfers are much more focused on analyzing the specific elements required to be effective in the sport, while others are more tuned in to the social context that the sport provides. Again, understand who you are, and have the flexibility and balance to express your style in preparation and training.

Detailers and Generalizers

Another MBTI personality dimension differentiates the more factual, detail-oriented, specific-minded individual from the more intuitive, general, possibilities-minded, big-picture type. Are you a detailer or a generalizer?

Detail-oriented golfers can be exacting, and they tend to focus on small imperfections. They enjoy creating and maintaining order. As part of their preparation, they often break down the performance of specific tasks and can easily incorporate these elements into their mental rehearsal. They may consider in detail how they will perform each element. However, they can get too focused on detail and overly upset by minor imperfections in their performance. At those times, they should be encouraged to step back, take a breath, and not lose sight of what they are trying to accomplish.

Generalizers focus on the big picture. They read overall patterns and frequently skip over minor details. If you are coaching a generalizer, remember that they might benefit by bringing a sharper, more detailed focus to their perspective and imagery. A good suggestion for a generalizer is to go back to those days when they really excelled and reflect on what they did to prepare and perform. Golfers who are more introverted and more task- and detail-oriented are more likely than extroverted generalizers to approach self-evaluation with interest, and their self-evaluation is apt to be more thorough.

To illustrate individual differences, here is a contrast between two golfers: Paul, who is an extrovert, feeling, generalizer-type golfer; and Harvey, who is a more introverted, thinking, detail-type golfer. Both enjoy the game.

Paul is outgoing, talkative, says what he's going to do that day on the course, warms up a little, nothing too specific, and, when he's ready, wants to get on with it. He often talks as he plays. When I asked Paul to write out his pre-shot routine, he said, "It's fairly straightforward. Can I just tell you what it is? Okay, first I take a breath, then I visualize the shot I want to make. I see the target, the trajectory of the ball flying toward the target. Then I take a couple of practice swings, step up, and make a smooth swing and hit a great shot." Paul is pleased with his good shots, visibly and verbally disappointed with the poor shots. He enjoys attention and approval.

Harvey is quiet. He takes warm-up very seriously and methodically appears to go through most of the clubs in his bag. When he is fully warmed up and tuned in to his satisfaction, he moves to the first tee. When I asked Harvey to describe his pre-shot routine, he wrote the following: "I always start by standing about 10 feet behind the ball and identifying the target line from me to my target. I imagine it as a continuous white line with an intermediate spot, usually a grass blemish, a few feet in front of the ball on that line." He added, "By bringing the target closer . . . like to that grass blemish it's easier to line things up. Then I imagine seeing the ball leave my club face toward the target. Next, stepping to my left into a parallel-left line, like train tracks to that imaginary target line, and at the same distance behind the ball, I take 2 full, smooth practice swings. As I take those practice swings, I continue to maintain the image of the ball tracking along the trajectory of the shot I've selected and 'see' it finish on the ground where I want it to finish.

"Then, still holding the same image, I set up to the ball. I set the club face behind the ball along the target line and then at the blemish spot and then aligning my body along the parallel-left line, ensuring my shoulders, knees, and feet are square to the ball/target line. I try not to feel tension, especially in my grip and my arms-to-shoulders, while waggling slowly three times. Then it's go-time. I see myself making a full, smooth swing. The pace of the swing being a 1+2 tempo with the accent on the '2' gradually increasing in speed reaching a crescendo through impact."

Then Harvey said, "I have a feeling I may have omitted to include something."

Clearly, there is a marked difference in understanding and focus between Paul and Harvey. Both are keen golfers.

In coaching Paul, it might be advisable to bring a little more specificity to his practice while still keeping it fluid and athletic. In coaching Harvey, it might be advisable to work at learning to release the excessive attention to detail and simply trust the feeling of his full, smooth swing.

TEST OF ATTENTIONAL AND INTERPERSONAL STYLE (TAIS)

The Test of Attentional and Interpersonal Style (TAIS) is another personality style inventory that differentiates the way people focus. The test defines two basic dimensions of focusing style: internal to external focus and broad to narrow focus. Healthy individuals have the capacity to shift to all four focusing styles (broad-external, broad-internal, narrow-external, narrow-internal) depending on the task required. For example, a narrow-external focus might be most effective in working on improving putting. And a narrow-internal focusing style might be utilized in doing some pre-match relaxing imagery.

What's your focusing style? Externally focused golfers tend to attend more to things happening around them (e.g., circumstances both in and around the match, the golf course, the leaderboard, the weather, the gallery, opponents, and teammates). They may pay less attention to how they feel and what's going on inside them. Often, they are not especially attuned to or accomplished at knowing when and how to pump themselves up or calm down.

Alternatively, there are those players who are more internally focused. Although they may have a clear idea of how they feel, they may be less cognizant of what is going on in the competition around them. In addition, width of focus can vary from broad to narrow. Players with too broad an external focus may be easily distracted and may react to anything or everything going on around them. Players with a narrow internal focus have a tendency to become overly self-reflective and excessively focused on their anxieties, aches, and pains. Golfers' focusing styles can affect how they manage themselves and their coachability.

COACHING INDIVIDUAL DIFFERENCES

Coaching is both an opportunity and a challenge to understand the marked range of personality differences that exist among golfers. Of course, the same differences that exist among golfers can also be found among coaches. Coaches can be introverted or extroverted, feeling- or task-oriented, detail people or generalizers, and internally or externally focused. An effective coach is one who knows his own style and predispositions and can understand and relate to athletes of all styles.

A coach's personality style can interact with a player's personality. For example, an extroverted coach may more readily understand the needs of an extroverted golfer — what makes him or her tick and how best to communicate with and coach that individual. To be effective, however, with an introverted golfer, the extroverted coach must adjust an energized and sometimes challenging or even confrontational style to the more sensitive personality style of the introverted golfer.

An introverted coach is likely to have some of the same control preferences as the introverted athlete and may be challenged to display the necessary flexibility in dealing with a more outgoing, spontaneous, extroverted athlete. Similarly, the very analytic, task-oriented coach may have a greater understanding of, and ability to communicate with, a task-oriented athlete and may find it more challenging to give encouraging emotional support to the feeling-type golfer. A coach who is more detail-oriented may need to be less detailed with players who are generalizers and yet help them appreciate the value of greater exactness in their preparation. Indeed, whenever there are personality style or communication differences between athlete and coach, both parties would be well advised to take a breath or two and exercise a little more patience and flexibility.

Whether you are a coach or a golfer, the ideal is to continuously assess and adjust. Get in touch with who you are, and learn how to create the feelings and thoughts that help you get into your optimal zone. Clearly, differing personality styles do this in different ways. And there are different ways to coach players to help them perform at their best.

TRAINING EXERCISES

1. Reflect on your personality style. Are you more of an extrovert or an introvert; thinking person or feeling person; a specific, detail-oriented person or a generalizer; more internally or externally focused?

   Understand that most of us have elements of both extremes in our personalities. If one element is clearly dominant, then reflect on your preparation and consider what adjustments you may need to make to help you prepare and perform consistently well. Depending on circumstance, sometimes it's advisable to talk with the coach and let them know what kind of support works best for you.

2. Whatever your personality type, practice improves performance and confidence. For the next month, before each practice, select a specific skill that you are going to work on to improve. Before practice, write down what drills you might do to improve that skill. After practice, note any observations you've made.

3. Journaling can be informative of patterns and areas of your preparation, performance, and lifestyle that need adjustment. Try keeping a golf journal for the next month.

CHAPTER THIRTEEN

Transferring Mental Skills

Right Focus, *Right Feeling*, and *Right Attitude* are three keys to performing well in any endeavor, especially in a psychophysical challenging sport like golf. Over the years, I have worked with over 40 sports at an elite level. A sport like Olympic shooting is an individual sport that demands considerable precision and emotional control, as does golf. In contrast, ice hockey and football are high-speed, physical, contact team sports. However, in hockey and football, as well as in golf, the same three keys are critical to consistent high-level performance.

HOCKEY TO GOLF

In the course of researching this book, I spoke with three former NHL clients who played professional hockey at the highest level for many years. They were all players I worked with on the mental game for several seasons, and they are now keen golfers. The question I asked them was if and how the mental work we did when they were playing hockey has helped their golf game. And if they had any insights they might share with interested golfers looking to improve their game.

Cliff Ronning

Cliff Ronning played 18 seasons and 1200 games in the NHL (with the St. Louis Blues, Vancouver Canucks, Nashville Predators, Minnesota Wild, LA Kings, and the New York Islanders). In recent years, Cliff has become a keen recreational golfer. I asked him to comment on if and how he was applying some of the mental work we did in hockey to playing golf.

Cliff: "Managing your emotions is more important in golf than in hockey. You have to stay quiet playing golf . . . and be more patient than in hockey. In hockey, if you get frustrated, you can cross-check someone. In golf, if you get upset after a bad shot, your game can go sideways quickly . . . and you could end up with a triple bogie.

"Playing with friends for fun is one thing. But when it's serious competition, and I'm playing the rules . . . something kicks in for me and all the things I learned playing hockey about managing emotions and dealing with pressure come into play. That's the breathing, taking a breath, 'changing the channel,' tuning out the negatives, talking positive to myself, using visualization to see the shot I want to make, and keeping my mind on the task at hand . . . plus staying in my routine. Those things all help me to have a little more confidence standing over the ball . . . and that's important."[1]

Morris Lukowich

Morris Lukowich played professional hockey for a dozen years in the NHL, with the Winnipeg Jets, Boston Bruins, and LA Kings; and in the WHA, with the Houston Aeros. In recent years, Morris has become an excellent golfer. I asked him to comment on if and how he was applying some of the mental techniques we worked with in hockey to playing golf.

First of all, Morris had some opinions about the title of this book: "I think a good title would be: *Winning Golf = Thinking + Being.* I love winning golf. Every weekend warrior wants to win, no matter at what level they play. Even if they're shooting 120 . . . then 118 is a win. And I think the second part of the title should be *Thinking + Being* because those are two key elements of the mental game."

Morris went on to say "The training we did has helped me more with the being part than the thinking part. That's because for the most part, I know what distance I can get from the various clubs. I know how to hit a draw, a fade, how to chip, and how to read a putt. So, making thinking decisions is pretty straightforward. I do use techniques you taught me in the thinking aspect, like positive self-talk and positive visualization. Before I hit a shot, I toss some grass in the air to see which way the wind is blowing, then I visualize the shot I want to make. I clearly imagine seeing the ball in the air, landing, then rolling toward the target.

"It's in the being aspect where the work we did has really been helpful . . . both before and after the shot.

"Before the shot, the breathing work helps me to relax. Relaxation is important because tension can ruin shots. I have a system for being with the club: As I get set, I take a breath, and as I breathe out, I say 'yes' and give the club a squeeze and relax my grip tension a little. I found that relaxing the grip leads to a better shot. I call this grip 'the Goldilocks grip,' not too hot, not too cold, but just right. Then I breathe in as I take the club back . . . and on the outbreath I say 'swing' and hit the ball. (Breathing out on the swing feels the same as when I was shooting the puck playing hockey.)

"After the shot the mental coaching we did has helped me deal with a bad shot. Something I've found to be challenging in golf is having to let go of the negativity when I'm walking to the ball after a bad shot . . . so that when I get up to the next shot, I'm ready to think and perform positively. For many years, I would condemn myself after a bad shot. Now, if I hit a bad shot, I use the release reflex technique we worked with and I'm able to release negativity, 'change the channel,' take a breath, and ask myself, 'What's the lesson to be learned? Why did I miss the shot — did my head move? Or did I do something else?' Then, I express gratitude for the awareness, forgive myself . . . and get ready to hit the next shot. *The key is learning how to change the irritation of a bad shot into the inspiration for the next shot.*"

I like Morris's phrasing "changing irritation into inspiration." As he said, "The way to do that is to change the channel, 'to re-lease' negative or anxious thoughts and feelings, and introduce something positive." Morris is very interested in how language empowers athletes and coaches. Expanding on the release reflex training we did when he was a player, Morris said, "*Re-lease* is an interesting word and process! In the word 're-lease' we get a new or second option on life. And the second option is to experience real ease or relative ease . . . and ease contributes to playing in the zone." He continued, "The process of *re-leasing* involves taking in a breath, and on the outbreath saying 'I can be better,' then focusing my thoughts on something that makes me smile."[2]

Be creative. Adapt the three-part release reflex to your game: *release tension* (negativity, frustration, anxiety), *breathe in* energy (which clears the mind), *refocus* (introduce a positive thought or feeling), and then bring that *state of being* to the next shot.

> "The whole secret to mastering the game of golf – and this applies to the beginner as well as the pro – is to cultivate a mental approach to the game that will enable you to shrug off the bad days (or bad shots), keep patient, and know in your heart that sooner or later you will be back on top."[3] – Arnold Palmer

Again, I like Morris's expression of the process of changing irritation to inspiration — it's a key to success on the golf course, and it's a key to experiencing more pleasure in life.

Bret Hedican

Bret Hedican played 17 seasons and over 1100 games in the NHL with the St. Louis Blues, Vancouver Canucks, Florida Panthers, Carolina Hurricanes, and Anaheim Ducks. In recent years, Bret has become a serious student of kung fu and a keen recreational golfer and fitness advisor. I asked Bret to comment on how he was applying some of the mental work we did in hockey to playing golf.

Bret mentioned that he had been helping a couple of young professional golfers who had been playing on Mackenzie (Canadian) and Korn Ferry (American) Tours. Along with coaching them on their fitness, Bret talked with them about the importance of doing mental reps, learning to slow breathing down, and experience some high-performance visualization. He also spoke with them about choosing an animal, a predator image that would be there for them when they stepped onto the first tee. Bret said, "I've talked with them about the feelings I had when I was playing hockey, crossing that threshold, climbing over the boards and stepping onto the ice, and becoming somebody else . . . a tiger, a hunter. And how they could get an edge doing that when they stepped onto the first tee. To really excel become the predator, become a hunter . . . hunting pars and birdies."

Bret explained, "I don't think golfers really understand the idea of mental reps. They think if they are putting in hours and hours on the range and visualizing their shots, they are doing mental reps. Those are physical reps. Mental reps are when you go home, in the evening or the afternoon, and you spend 15 to 20 minutes by yourself, and you slow your breathing down, and you reflect on your strengths as a golfer — who you are — and you see yourself walking the golf course, and you see yourself making shots." He continued, "Learning to create good feelings creates good thoughts, and those good thoughts create more good feelings. Those are mental reps."

Bret went on to say that for young golfers, searching for ways to be better, working on their mental game is one place where they can really improve their golf performance. He related that one golfer he had been coaching had a poor start in a couple of tournaments and how he's learned to turn that around. Bret reported, "He's learning to 'change the channel' and stay in the moment. He now has a lot better self-talk and he's doing a lot more mental reps, and because of it, he's having success." He continued, "Something I emphasize is that changing one's mental game isn't going to happen overnight. It's the same as if you were to walk into the gym, hire a trainer, and on the first day he gives you 225 pounds to bench press . . . and you've never lifted weights. Trying to lift that weight you could end up crushing your chest. You're not going to see success moving that bar, getting it off the rack. It may take months, or years, before you could bench press that weight. But if you work out every day and get stronger and stronger, eventually you can press the weight." Bret added, "If you don't do your reps regularly, how do you expect it to lift 225? My point is that it's the very same with mental reps. It takes time and dedication . . . and doing your mental reps every day can change your game."

I told Bret I completely agree. I always tell my clients that I know if I go to the gym and lift weights, I get stronger. However, knowing this and not doing the work changes nothing. And going once or twice changes very little. It's the focused dedication, the deliberate practice of good physical and *mental* techniques, that builds results. Across sport, people give more credence to doing the physical reps than to doing the mental training.

Bret continued, "One other thing I wanted to relate was that one of my golf students has led in a couple of tournaments . . . but then faded late in the final round. I started changing the way he trains both physically and mentally. I did a heart rate test with him and I had him do a Dorsey Flex Jump test for three minutes and measured his heart rate. Now, this is a very stressful test and his heart rate should have been at a maximum. I was shocked his was only 130 . . . which is quite low for a serious young athlete in his mid-twenties. The problem is he's never done any high-end physical training where his heart rate has approached 160. My point with this is I believe he has to learn to train physically much harder in order to get his heart rate higher. Otherwise, on a Sunday afternoon, when he's leading a tournament and the adrenaline is flowing and his heart rate is at 150 (and in training his max heart rate is only 130), he is well beyond the rate his heart is comfortable functioning at. Consequently, he is stressing physiologically, and it's more difficult for him to use his breathing to calm down. Something I helped him to understand is that he needs to do some physical training at a higher intensity level.

"Saul, in your book I think you need to talk about heart rate. One thing golfers have to deal with is performing well under pressure. I remember being in game 7 of the Stanley Cup finals, and I remember the intense pressure of playing in the playoffs. I was able to use my breathing to calm down because my conditioning had been intense and my heart rate was used to being pretty high when adrenaline was flowing. And I was always able to use my breathing to bring my heart rate down which enabled me to play better. A key to performing well under pressure is connecting my mind and body together. I used it in those big games on the ice . . . and I use it playing golf. And that's what I try to teach these young golfers to connect their mind and body through their breath . . . and with their heart rate."

I replied, "Bret, this is interesting stuff. You're saying that if you train physically with enough intensity to increase the range of your heart rate, then you will be more comfortable and better able to manage your feelings when you are in a pressure situation, especially when adrenaline is flowing, like in the final round of a golf match. Of course, being in excellent shape makes good sense. Adding some intensity training to elevate heart rate in order to give you a broader 'comfort-management-zone' is an interesting performance concept."[4]

So, readers, check with your health professional as to what would be a healthy accelerated heart rate for you, and incorporate that knowledge into adjusting your intensity training accordingly.

FOOTBALL TO GOLF

After talking with several hockey veterans, I asked a couple of my former NFL clients if and how they were applying the mental techniques we worked with when they were playing football to improve their golf game.

LeRoy Irvin

LeRoy Irvin was an NFL All-Pro cornerback with the Los Angeles Rams. In his 11 NFL seasons, his challenge was to cover some of pro football's fastest and best wide receivers, and also to step up and stop the run. As he put it, "I'm a man on an island. I'm on my own out there. Everyone can see me, but no one can help me." (I'm sure a lot of golfers have had that very same thought.) A mistake, a lapse, a slip could mean a touchdown. To my mind his is one of the more challenging jobs in pro sport.

LeRoy asked me for something that could give him an edge, keep him loose and focused, and help him deal with the pressure play after play. We worked with his breathing, so that between plays he could draw in the power of the waves and combine that good feeling with positive thoughts like "I'm in charge" and "the force is with me."

LeRoy has become a good recreational golfer. When I reconnected with him after a couple of decades, he was playing in a charity golf tournament. I explained that I was writing a book on the mental side of golf and was curious if he was using any of the good focus, good feeling techniques we worked with when he was playing in the NFL.

"I still think about the sessions we had with the Rams and how it helped me to stay in the moment and be consistent . . . like the waves," LeRoy said. "And in my golf game it's also about being consistent like the waves . . . about forgetting the last shot. It's all about the new shot coming up and focusing on the now. When I'm playing golf, I'm really trying to relax my mind, staying in the now . . . and the breathing keeps me there."

He continued, "In football when I was covering someone and I got beat on a bad play, I used to take it so seriously. In the sessions we had, you taught me I can't think about the last play, or the last wave. We talked about relaxing, breathing, and being in the now. I try to think that way in my life. It's especially helpful in golf, where every shot is new and different. So, I just want to be in the now, stay with the waves. I try to get all the negative stuff out with the breathing . . . breathe out the negative thoughts, and breathe in the positive."

"The breathing thing is so simple and helpful," I responded. "I work with a lot of good young athletes — 16, 17, 18 years old. They want to play pro: hockey, baseball, golf, or whatever. They come to me because they want to be the best they can be at their sport. Talking with their parents, I sometimes explain that the techniques their children are learning to improve at their sport apply to everything in life.

"It's like you said, LeRoy: We get focused on negative things from the past . . . or we worry about stuff from the future . . . and the power is in the present, so get back to the waves. The waves are now."

LeRoy continued, "Golf is such a mental game. It really is. And you don't play against a person. You play against the golf course, something that's not even alive . . . but it's sitting there breathing down your throat. In football, you're playing against a guy. And if you are more physical and more prepared than the guy you're against, you're going to beat him. But in golf you are playing against the golf course, your emotions, and the pressure of the moment."

I replied, "Yes, and the ball you're playing with has no energy of its own. It gets its energy from you. So, get into the flow. Create the good focus and the good feeling. Feel energy flowing to you and through you. Tension and negativity interrupt the flow. So, for best results, use the breathing to keep energy flowing to you and through you."

I mentioned to LeRoy that in the book I talked with two pro golfers who shot 55, the best score ever for a round on a regulation golf course. And something that stood out about their performance was they were playing a recreational round; they were feeling good, enjoying themselves. They had good focus, good feeling, and a good attitude. They just believed they could make their shots. When we start fighting against the ball, the course, ourselves, or against anybody else, we tighten up and performance drops. It's always back to the waves, back to the breath.

LeRoy agreed. "Yes, that's true a hundred percent, in football, in golf . . . and in life."[5]

Mark Jerue

Mark Jerue was a linebacker and an intense competitor who played seven seasons in the NFL, with the Los Angeles Rams. I was asked to develop a program for him that he could use to deal with a specific performance issue. Mark would get so intense in games that he would develop game-limiting cramps. The first season we worked together on conscious breathing, tension-release techniques, and mental rehearsal. The next year he became a starter and he wanted something to help him from getting too intense. He specifically wanted to have more control of his emotions, to focus more clearly on task requirements, to make the right reads, and to be able to react at his best play after play.

I developed a special mnemonic program for Mark. Before every play, Mark would think, "A, B, C, D, E, F, G, H." "A, B, C" was A=always, B=breathe, and C=be calm. As soon as the previous play was over, Mark would think "A, B, C," take a few breaths, and calm down. Then, a little more at ease and possessing the judgment that calmness can provide, he'd switch his focus externally to the task at hand and think "D, E, F, G, H." The "D" meant down and distance (e.g., second down and seven yards to go, or third down and five yards to go). The "E" meant evaluate. Mark would consider the probabilities of what the opposition was likely to do in that situation. The "F" referred to the formation (e.g., two wide receivers right, or two tight ends in, or wide receiver left). Each formation cued Mark to specific responsibilities. Then, Mark would think "G" for guard. He'd cue the guard's stance for pass or run probabilities. Last, Mark would think "H" for hit, which meant intensify emotion and be ready for war. The program matched his focusing needs and worked extremely well. The "A, B, C, D, E, F, G, H" mnemonic was simple enough to remember even under the intense emotion of an NFL game, and it gave Mark the ability to regulate his feelings and to focus on the key externals to be effective.

It's been over two decades since Mark retired, and in that time, he has become a business success and a good recreational golfer. I thought it would be interesting to see if Mark was using any of the mental techniques we worked with when he was playing in the NFL to improve his golf game. When I asked him, he said he did do some breathing to be calm, as well as some positive visualization. Then, on reflection, Mark added that maybe doing more mental work could have a positive impact on his golf game. I reminded Mark about the "A, B, C, D, E, F, G, H" technique we used years before.[6]

Recalling that program, I thought it might be a good idea to create a similar mnemonic approach to help golfers develop an effective pre-swing routine. So here it is: take a breath, assess the situation, then it's I, F, A — B, S, T, where I=imagine (envision the shot you want to make), F=feel it (take a practice swing re-creating the feeling you've had when you've made similar shots), A=approach (step up to the ball), B=breathe easy, S=swing (smooth and strong), T=target (see the ball go to your target).

To remember the letters I, F, A, B, S, and T, create a mnemonic device, a phrase or sentence that incorporates them such as "Imagine Feeling A Better Swing Today." Repeat that sentence. Anybody can remember a simple, positive sentence like "Imagine feeling a better swing today," and thinking it can remind you to have a focused, good-feeling pre-swing routine.

Be creative. If you prefer, develop your own pre-swing elements and a mnemonic that goes with them to give you more focus, feel, and consistency. And, of course, feel free to adapt any of the techniques described in *Winning Golf* to give you more impact and pleasure playing the game of golf . . . and in life.

CHAPTER SUMMARIES

Chapter One: Mapping Out the Mental Game

"Golf is 90 percent mental and the other 10 percent is mental too."
— Jim Flick

Golf is a very mental sport. The mind is an amazing supercomputer . . . and you are the boss. You are "response-able" to create the feelings, focus, and attitude that will enable you to perform well. Set some SMART (Specific, Measurable, Attainable, Relevant, Timely) golf goals.

Chapter Two: The Problem

"The mind messes up more shots than the body." — Tommy Bolt

Golfers often experience problems caused by anxiety, tension, trying too hard, and thinking too much. One of the keys to playing better golf is learning to relax under pressure; relaxation brings more ease and fluidity to one's swing. Experience *right feeling* and *right focus*.

Chapter Three: Managing Emotions – Conscious Breathing

"When I learned how to breathe, I learned how to win." — Tom Watson

Managing emotions is vital to playing consistently well. One key to quieting the mind is *conscious breathing*. The technique (rhythm, inspiration, direction) is described in detail in this chapter.

Chapter Four: Changing Programs – The Release Reflex

"You can talk strategy all you want, but what really matters is resiliency."
— Hale Irwin

The *release reflex* explains how to change programs and let go of tense, anxious, negative thoughts and feelings, and tune in to right feelings and right focus.

Chapter Five: Power Thinking

"As an athlete, as a competitor, you have to have that belief in yourself."
— Tiger Woods

Power thinking involves technical thoughts, strategy thoughts, and personal thoughts. Know you are a good player and know your strengths. Use power words and golf affirmations to build and reinforce a positive sense of self.

Chapter Six: High-Performance Imagery

"Visualization is the most powerful thing we have." — Nick Faldo

Imagery can be a powerful aid to your golf. Use goal imagery, stimulating imagery, and mental rehearsal to improve your game. Be the tiger or the eagle on the tee and on the green.

Chapter Seven: Exceptional Performances – The Sub-60 Club

"I felt invincible, almost like I knew when I was standing over some of the putts, I just knew that it was going to go in the hole. It was a momentous round. I made a birdie, I made an eagle, I made a birdie and another birdie. My performance was always there." — Rhein Gibson

"I always believed I could birdie every hole. Growing up in Sweden we had something called Vision 54 . . . kind of a mental vision [program] as to how to play really good golf. It always talked about what it would feel like to hit every green. What it would feel like to make every putt. So, the question is, why can't you do it in one round? I always believed that it was possible."

— Annika Sorenstam

Chapter Eight: Commitment

"Your success only makes you more motivated to be better. My lowest score here is 64 and I'd love to better that." — Rory McIlroy

How committed are you to becoming the best golfer you can be? If the goal is to be the best, then whatever comes up, *use it*. If you play well, *use it* to build your confidence. If you play poorly, *use it* to improve your process. If you don't use it, it will use you. Perseverance and discipline are expressions of commitment.

Chapter Nine: Confidence

"Confidence is king in golf." — Jason Dufner

"Confidence is the most important single factor in this game, and no matter how great your natural talent, there is only one way to obtain it and sustain it: WORK." — Jack Nicklaus

Confidence is a key to performing consistently well. *Success* builds confidence. And so does *preparation*.

Chapter Ten: Identity

"I think the game of golf teaches you so much about yourself, like who you really are and what you are made of." — Stewart Cink

A positive golf identity is another key to confidence and consistent high-level performance. Pride, love, and a sense of deserving can all build a strong golf identity.

Chapter Eleven: Balance and Lifestyle

"Going to the gym is great for your body but it's also great for your mind."
— Rory McIlroy

"Keep your sense of humor. There is enough stress in the rest of your life to not let bad shots ruin a game you're supposed to enjoy." — Amy Alcott

Balance and a healthy lifestyle support good health and good performance. This chapter looks at diet, exercise, R&R, relationships, attitude, and gratitude.

Chapter Twelve: Individual Differences

"Pressure creates tension and, when you are tense, you want to get the task over as fast as possible. The more you hurry in golf, the worse you probably will play, which leads to heavier pressure and even greater tension. To avoid this vicious circle, I'll take a few deep breaths and quickly review why I'm doing what I'm doing." — Jack Nicklaus

"The pressure makes me more intent on each shot. Pressure on the last few holes makes me play better." — Nancy Lopez

Personality differences exist among golfers. What's interesting is how these differences affect preparation and performance. There are a number of factors that can account for the different ways people react to pressure. A few of the more relevant differences in personality style to consider are introversion vs extroversion, task-orientation (analytical, thinking) vs feeling-orientation (intuitive, social), detail orientation (specifics) vs general orientation ("big picture"), focus style (external, internal, broad, narrow).

Chapter Thirteen: Transferring Mental Skills

"The key is learning how to change the irritation of a bad shot into the inspiration for the next shot." — Morris Lukowich

An examination of professional athletes transferring mental skills learned playing in the NHL and NFL to playing better golf.

THE REMARKABLE CAST
OF CHARACTERS IN
WINNING GOLF:
THE MENTAL GAME

Stuart Appleby (Australia): A multiple PGA Tour winner and member of the "sub-60 club."

Tommy Armour (Scotland): Nicknamed "The Silver Scot," he was one of the legendary players of the first half of the 20th century. A winner of three Majors and author of one of the classic golf instruction books, *How to Play Your Best Golf All the Time* (1953).

Paul Azinger (USA): Current NBC TV golf commentator; a former prolific PGA Tour winner, including the 1993 PGA Championship; and successful U.S. Ryder Cup team captain.

Seve Ballesteros (Spain): Winner of five Majors and 90 worldwide professional titles, including a World No.1 Hall of Fame. Seve was a perennial Ryder Cup star and major influence on the development of European professional golf.

Chip Beck (USA): Member of the "sub-60 club" and a successful player on the PGA Tour in the 1980s and 1990s.

Tom Blanckaert (Belgium): Noted PGA Teaching Professional.

Tommy Bolt (USA): The 1958 U.S. Open champion and winner of 15 PGA Tour events.

Brad Bryant (USA): Longtime PGA Tour player, who made his biggest mark on the PGA Champions Tour.

Mark Calcavecchia (USA): The 1989 British Open winner, 1990s Ryder Cup stalwart, and multiple winner on the PGA Tour.

Billy Casper (USA): Winner of two U.S. Opens (1959 and 1966) and the 1970 Masters, plus numerous PGA Tour and Champions Tour wins. In total, Billy won 51 PGA Tour events and is considered the best putter of his era.

Stewart Cink (USA): The 2009 British Open champion, winner of several PGA Tour titles (Rookie of the Year 1997), and U.S. Ryder Cup team member.

Corey Connors (Canada): A PGA Tour winner, noted for consistently contending in Tour and Major events and considered to have one of the finer swings in the game.

Bruce Crampton (Australia): Won 45 times as a professional — 14 on the PGA Tour, and later dominated the Champions Tour with 20 wins.

Ben Crenshaw (USA): "Gentle Ben" was noted for his modest demeanor. A protégé of Harvey Penick, he was twice the Masters Champion (1984 and 1995). He's also acclaimed for his many Ryder Cup performances (U.S. Ryder Cup captain in 1999) and for his putting prowess.

Brian Danny (Canada): Former club golf champion and founder of the first international chapter of The First Tee.

Bryson DeChambeau (USA): U.S. Open winner 2020, and eight PGA Tour events. He is the longest driver in history of the Tour and is famous for his extreme analytical approach to the golf swing.

Jason Dufner (USA): PGA Tour Champion 2013.

David Duval (USA): Member of the "59 club" and winner of 13 PGA Tour titles between 1997 and 2000 (including the 1998 Players Championship and 1999 British Open). A former World No. 1, and a Golf Channel commentator.

Steve Elkington (Australia): Noted for his elegant swing. PGA Champion 1995, and winner of 10 Tour titles (including two Players Championships).

Ernie Els (South Africa): Considered an all-time great, with 74 worldwide wins and a former World No. 1. Winner of two U.S. Opens and 2 British Opens. Nicknamed "The Big Easy" for his size, effortless swing, and easy-going demeanor.

Sir Nick Faldo (England): One of the game's all-time greats and former World No. 1. A six-time Major Champion (three Masters and three British Opens) and leading TV commentator.

Tony Finau (USA): PGA Tour player and winner.

Jack Fleck (USA): Winner of the 1955 U.S. Open, having defeated the famed Ben Hogan in a playoff.

Jim Flick (USA): Renowned American golf instructor and author of many articles on the game, mainly with *Golf Digest*. Jim became Jack Nicklaus's coach later in the latter's career.

Rickie Fowler (USA): Winner of five PGA Tour titles, including The Players in 2015. A former U.S. Ryder Cup and Presidents Cup team member.

Jim Furyk (USA): The 2003 U.S. Open Champion and only two-time member of the "sub-60 club," including the lowest score ever on Tour (58); 2010 FedEx Champion and PGA Tour Player of the Year. A perennial Ryder Cup team member and captain in 2018. Jim had 28 total professional wins.

Sergio Garcia (Spain): Won the Masters in 2017 and has a total of 36 victories worldwide. He was in the top ten of the Official World Golf Rankings for 450 weeks, and has been a European Ryder Cup fixture throughout his career.

Al Geiberger (USA): The Original "Mr. 59," the first one to break 60 in the PGA Tour, in 1975. Al was PGA Tour Champion in 1966, and has won 30 professional titles.

Rhein Gibson (Australia): PGA and Korn Ferry Tour player, holder of the Guinness World Record for lowest score ever (55) on a regulation golf course.

Forrest Gregg (USA): NFL Hall of Fame football player, and later an NFL football coach.

Adam Hadwin (Canada): Member of the "sub-60 club" and a PGA Tour winner.

Arnold Haultain: Author of the 1908 classic *The Mystery of Golf* — "no one has come closer than Haultain to explaining the ultimate riddle of the game."

Bret Hedican (USA): NHL veteran of 17 seasons, who played in 1100 games.

Brooke Henderson (Canada): One of the longest hitters on the LPGA Tour and one of the most consistent players. Brooke won the 2016 Women's PGA Championship and 14 professional tournaments.

Ben Hogan (USA): A true legend, he is universally ranked in the top three of all time. He won four U.S. Opens, the only British Open he entered, two Masters and two PGA Championship and 64 PGA Tour events. Ben is famous for his dedication to practice and the principles of the golf swing, having authored the all-time best-selling instructional book, *Ben Hogan's Five Lessons: The Modern Fundamentals of Golf.*

Max Homa (USA): PGA Tour rising star, NCAA champion, recent PGA Tour winner. Wells Fargo Championship 2019, Genesis Invitational 2021.

Alexander Hughes (USA): PGA golfer who tied with Rhein Gibson for the Guinness World Records' lowest score ever (55) on a regulation golf course.

Mackenzie Hughes (Canada): PGA Tour winner, former two-time Canadian amateur Champion (2011 and 2012).

LeRoy Irvin (USA): NFL all-pro cornerback, 11 seasons.

Hale Irwin (USA): Three-time U.S. Open Champion, winner of 83 professional titles, including most Champions Tour wins (45), member of five winning U.S. Ryder Cup teams.

Mark Jerue (USA): NFL veteran linebacker, seven seasons.

Dustin Johnson (USA): U.S. Open Champion 2016, Masters Champion 2020, winner of 24 PGA Tour titles, and FedEx Cup Champion 2020. Dustin is arguably the straightest of the long-hitters on the PGA Tour and has developed a great short-game to go with that.

Bobby Jones (USA): In the 1920s, the four "Majors" were the U.S. and British Amateurs and Open Championships, and Jones won all four in one year. He was undisputedly the best player of his time but remained an "amateur." Forever the classic gentleman, Bobby Jones never turned professional. He co-founded Augusta National Golf Club and the Masters Tournament.

Danielle Kang (USA): LPGA Tour top-ranked player, 2017 Women's PGA Champion.

Ray Knight (USA): All-star MLB baseball infielder, 13 seasons, World Series MVP, 1986, and MLB manager and broadcaster.

Lydia Ko (New Zealand): Youngest golfer (aged 15) to win a professional tournament and World No. 1 ranking (held for 109 weeks). Only golfer to win two Olympic medals (Silver 2016 and Bronze 2021). Winner of 19 LPGA events, including two Majors.

Nelly Korda (USA): Olympic Gold medalist 2021, No. 1 ranked LPGA player, winner of six titles on the LPGA Tour and one on LET.

Matt Kuchar (USA): The 2012 Players Champion, a top-ten money-winning machine. Matt has had 17 professional wins.

David Leadbetter: One of world's best-known golf teachers, who worked with several of golf's top players — most famously known for rebuilding Nick Faldo's swing.

Greg LeMond (USA): First North American to win the Tour de France, and he did it three times.

Justin Leonard (USA): Twelve PGA Tour victories, including the 1997 U.S. Open and the 1998 Players Championship. Justin is a three-time Ryder Cup Team member.

Nancy Lopez (USA): One of the greatest LPGA Tour players ever. A member of the World Golf and LPGA Halls of Fame. Nancy won 48 LPGA tournaments, including three Majors. The Nancy Lopez Achievement Award is given to an LPGA pro who emulates qualities Nancy exemplified: leadership, passion, giving, and approachability.

Morris Lukowich (Canada): NHL and WHA veteran, 12 seasons.

Hideki Matsuyama (Japan): One of most successful Japanese players on the PGA Tour. Ranked World No. 2, after second place finish in 2017 U.S. Open.

Barry McDonnell (USA): PGA instructor instrumental in Rickie Fowler's formative years.

Jim Nelford (Canada): NCAA All American, was highly competitive on the PGA Tour (35 straight cuts) until a freak boating accident cut his career short. A former TV golf commentator and an innovative golf instructor, currently based in North Carolina.

Byron Nelson (USA): Won a record 11 PGA Tour events in a row in 1945, and 50 Tour events overall. His swing was so consistent that True Temper and USGA patterned and named their Swing Testing machine "Iron Byron" after him.

Jack Nicklaus (USA): "Golden Bear," arguably one of the greatest ever! Jack is the all-time record holder for most Major wins (18 — three more than Tiger Woods), with a total of 73 PGA Tour victories.

Moe Norman (Canada): Canadian Tour professional, who's considered to be one of the best ball-strikers ever among his peers. Moe was known for his unique one-plane swing and eccentric personality.

Mac O'Grady (USA): PGA Tour winner. Best known as an instructor to several Tour players.

Arnold Palmer (USA): "The King," with 64 PGA Tour wins, including four Masters, two British Opens, and the 1960 U.S. Open.

Bill Parcells (USA): Successful NFL football coach, who transformed 4 losing teams into winners (New York Giants, New York Jets, New England patriots, Dallas Cowboys).

Harvey Penick (USA): Coached several future Hall of Famers, including Ben Crenshaw and Tom Kite. Famous for authoring his *Little Red Book* of musings on the game.

Gary Player (South Africa): Nine-time Major winner and considered one of the best players ever.

Cliff Ronning (Canada): NHL veteran with 18 seasons and 1200 games.

Bob Rotella (USA): Sport psychologist and author of *Golf Is Not a Game of Perfect*.

Xander Schauffele (USA): World No. 4 and the 2021 Olympic Gold Medal. Winner of four events in first four years on PGA Tour, including the prestigious WGC (World Golf Championships — HSBC) and FedEx Tour Championship.

Scottie Scheffler (USA): The 2020 PGA Tour Rookie of the Year and a "59 club" member.

Scott Shelton (USA): former NCAA and PGA professional golfer.

Sam Snead (USA): A true legend of the game and winner of 7 Major titles and a record 82 PGA Tour titles (tied with Tiger Woods). "Slammin' Sammy" was known for his smooth swing and longevity in the game.

Annika Sorenstam (Sweden): All-time LPGA great, with over 90 wins worldwide. The only woman to break 60 (59). She won 10 Majors.

Roger Staubach (USA): NFL Hall of Fame football player.

Payne Stewart (USA): Three-time Majors Champion (1991 and 1999 U.S. Opens, 1989 PGA). His elegant swing and throwback stylish wardrobe defined him. Payne died young in a chartered-plane crash.

Curtis Strange (USA): Back-to-back U.S. Open winner (1988 and 1989). A former TV commentator and multiple PGA Tour winner.

Bob Toski (USA): A successful PGA Tour player in the 1950s. The smallest player on the PGA Tour, who later became one of the most respected golf instructors and had a long association with Jim Flick.

Yani Tseng (Taiwan): A dominant LPGA force — World No. 1 for 106 weeks. The youngest player, male or female, to win 5 Majors among her 27 tournaments worldwide.

Harry Vardon (England): Legendary six-time British Open Champion and 1900 U.S. Open winner. Famous for the "Vardon grip," which to this day is the "standard" method for holding the club.

Bill Walker (USA): A 90-year-old golfer who, at the time of writing *Winning Golf*, could shoot his age.

Eric Wang (USA, Canada): California native, and Korn Ferry and Canadian Tour player, and CPGA teaching professional at the Victoria Golf Academy in British Columbia.

Bubba Watson (USA): Two-time Masters Champion and winner of 12 Tour events. Bubba is one of a few left-handers on the Tour and one of the Tour's longest hitters.

Tom Watson (USA): Truly one of the all-time greats, with 70 worldwide wins, including eight Major titles: two Masters, one U.S. Open, and five British Opens.

Mike Weir (Canada): A left-handed player, Mike won the 2003 Masters and 8 PGA Tour events. He was ranked in the top ten in World rankings for 110 weeks, between 2001 and 2005.

Lee Westwood (England): The ultra-consistent Englishman has been one of the most international players and is considered "the best never to have won a Major," but with numerous close misses. European Ryder Cup star, with 44 worldwide wins.

Russell Wilson (USA): A football player — NFL all-pro quarterback.

Tiger Woods (USA): Arguably, the greatest ever. Tiger has changed the game and is an inspiration for many of the current generation's young stars. Tiger is the winner of 15 Majors — only 3 shy of Jack Nicklaus's record — and shares the record of 82 Tour wins with Sam Snead.

Richard Zokol (Canada): Dick was an NCAA All-American and a PGA Tour winner. He recently developed an app called MindTRAK Golf to assist golfers to focus on process and away from "problematic result-orientated mindsets."

ACKNOWLEDGMENTS

I wish to acknowledge the following individuals who helped make and shape *Winning Golf: The Mental Game* — Laara K. Maxwell, for her editorial acumen and sound advice; Brian Danny, a golf aficionado and friend, for numerous suggestions and steadfast support; Garfield L. Miller, my infrequent and favorite golf partner, for his sound advice whenever asked for; and Marty Wright, an old friend, for his advice (even when not asked for).

My sincere gratitude to a number of golfers who contributed directly to the book, sharing their experience and insights, including Rhein Gibson, Alexander Hughes, Nancy Lopez, Jim Nelford, Bill Walker, Eric Wang, and Dick Zokol. Thanks also to the many young golfers, collegiate golfers, and those trying to make it professionally, who I consulted with over the years and who taught me as much as I taught them. A special thanks to several of my former NHL and NFL clients who have become keen golfers — Bret Hedican, LeRoy Irvin, Mark Jerue, Morris Lukowich, and Cliff Ronning — who explained how the mental skills we worked on during their NHL and NFL careers contributed to their playing better golf.

I am grateful to the many remarkable golf professionals whose ideas and comments I have shared throughout the book. It's a long list that

ACKNOWLEDGMENTS

includes Amy Alcott, Stuart Appleby, Tommy Armour, Paul Azinger, Seve Ballesteros, Chip Beck, Tom Blanckaert, Tommy Bolt, Brad Bryant, Mark Calcavecchia, Billy Casper, Stewart Cink, Corey Conners, Bruce Crampton, Ben Crenshaw, Bryson DeChambeau, Jason Dufner, David Duval, Steve Elkington, Ernie Els, Nick Faldo, Tony Finau, Jim Flick, Ricky Fowler, Jim Furyk, Sergio Garcia, Al Geiberger, Adam Hadwin, Brooke Henderson, Ben Hogan, Max Homa, Mackenzie Hughes, Hale Irwin, Dustin Johnson, Bobby Jones, Danielle Kang, Lydia Ko, Brooks Koepka, Nelly Korda, Matt Kuchar, David Leadbetter, Justin Leonard, Davis Love Jr., Hideki Matsuyama, Barry McDonnell, Paul McGinley, Rory McIlroy, Phil Mickelson, Johnny Miller, Collin Morikawa, Byron Nelson, Jack Nicklaus, Greg Norman, Moe Norman, Arnold Palmer, Harvey Penick, Gary Player, Xander Schauffele, Scottie Scheffler, Scott Shelton, Sam Snead, Annika Sorenstam, Jordan Spieth, Payne Stewart, Curtis Strange, Justin Thomas, Bob Toski, Lee Trevino, Yani Tseng, Harry Vardon, Bubba Watson, Tom Watson, Mike Weir, Lee Westwood, and Tiger Woods.

I'd like to acknowledge a collection of athletes, coaches, writers, and politicians whom I quoted to illustrate a point: Calvin Coolidge, Albert Einstein, Tim Gallwey, Forrest Gregg, Arnold Haultain, Duncan Keith, Bobby Knight, Marcus Naslund, Bill Parcells, Bob Rotella, Roger Staubach, and Russell Wilson. Also, many thanks to Lorne Rubenstein and Sami Jo Small for suggesting ECW press.

Last, but by no means least, a heartfelt thank you to Shannon Parr, Jessica Albert, and the winning team at ECW, headed by Michael Holmes, a supportive editor, a keen golfer, and a good fellow.

209

NOTES

CHAPTER ONE: MAPPING OUT THE MENTAL GAME

1. Jim Flick and Jack Nicklaus, "Jim Flick And Jack Nicklaus: Go to The Movies," *Golf Digest*, April 27, 2010, golfdigest.com/story/flick-nicklaus-film.
2. PGA Tour, "Max Homa Talks Recent Mental Changes to Improve Life and Golf," Facebook, January 23, 2021, facebook.com/page/10643196329/search/?q=Perspective.
3. Quotefancy (website), accessed January 5, 2022, quotefancy.com/greg-norman-quotes.
4. Beth Ann Nichols, "'It Wasn't Really a Break': Danielle Kang among Headliners at LPGA Opener after Short, Hectic Offseason," *Golfweek*, January 19, 2021, golfweek.usatoday.com/2021/01/19/danielle-kang-lpga-tournament-champions-preview.

CHAPTER TWO: THE PROBLEM

1. Arnold Palmer — Baylife, March 2015, #5.
2. Brainy Quote (website), "Ernie Els Quotes," accessed January 5, 2022, brainyquote.com/authors/ernie-els-quotes.

3. Pinterest (website), accessed January 5, 2022, pinterest.com/pin/562897965342o069041.

4. The-Golf-Experience (website), accessed January 5, 2022, the-golf-experience.com/sam-snead-quotes.html.

5. Quote Fancy (website), accessed January 5, 2022, quotefancy.com/jack-nicklaus-quotes.

6. Marty Wright, personal communication.

7. A-Z Quotes (website), accessed January 5, 2022, azquotes.com/quote/579505.

8. Adam Hadwin, "Adam Hadwin Thursday Flash Interview 2020 The Master Tournament — Round 1," November 12, 2020, YouTube video, youtube.com/watch?v=eo7Bz7wFrno.

9. Golf Australia, "Stuart Appleby Golf Tips — Getting Back onto the Fairway," April 16, 2012, YouTube video, youtube.com/watch?v=Sg-bKwnGk6M.

10. TenGolf, "Lydia Ko: Winner Press Conference 2021 LOTTE Championship LPGA Tour," April 18, 2021, YouTube video, youtube.com/results?search_query=v%3Dlu-KRFLu38E-Winner+press+Conference+2021+Lotte+Championship+LPGA+Tour.

11. Brian Danny, personal communication.

12. Jim Nelford, personal communication. See also Jim Nelford, "Jim Nelford Golf Clinic at Freedom Fairways, Sun City Center," August 20, 2014, YouTube video, youtube.com/watch?v=aeBjHdiPypI).

13. Associated Press, "Flick, One of Golf's Most Prolific and Influential Instructors, Dies at Age 82," November 5, 2012, pga.com/archive/jim-flick-one-golfs-most-prolific-and-influential-instructors-dies-age-82.

14. Farmers Insurance (website), "Rickie Fowler Learns the Hard Way, and It's Paying Off," accessed January 15, 2022, farmers.com/learn/real-stories/rickie-vs-rickie.

15. Verenda Smith, "'Shrink' Shrinks MSU Golf Scores," *The Clarion-Ledger*, April 26, 1981.

SECTION TWO: RIGHT FEELING

1. Jake Humphrey and Damian Hughes, hosts, "Paul McGinley: Empower Not Overpower," *The High Performance Podcast*, video podcast, August 9, 2021, youtube.com/watch?v=Gy85UTzRTG4.

CHAPTER THREE: MANAGING EMOTIONS – CONSCIOUS BREATHING

1. Epigraph: We Play Golf TV, Tom Blanckaert, "The Best Golf Tip Ever: Don't Forget to Breathe!" December 1, 2017, YouTube video, youtube.com/watch?v=SsR-AIrStho.

2. First to Tee, "Xander Schauffele, Tokyo 2020 Olympic Winner," August 1, 2021, YouTube video, youtube.com/watch?v=ixvonz Hwu6Q.

3. Quote Fancy (website), accessed January 15, 2022, quotefancy.com/ quote/1781537/Paul-Azinger-Staying-in-the-present-is-the-key-to-any-golfer-s-game-once-you-start.

4. Golf Channel, "Positive Nerves Push Collin Morikawa to Open Championship Victory," July 18, 2021, YouTube video, youtube.com/watch?v=vumRG6ILWBA.

5. Annika Foundation, "Live Lesson with Annika — Mental Game," April 27, 2020, facebook.com/watch/?v=1133207180365577.

6. Andrea Zaccaro, Andrea Piarulli, Marco Laurino, Erika Garbella, Danilo Menicucci, Bruno Neri, and Angelo Gemignani, "How Breath-Control Can Change Your Life: A Systematic Review on Psycho-Physical Correlates of Slow Breathing," *Frontiers in Human Neuroscience*, 07 September 2018, doi.org/10.3389/fnhum.2018.00353.

7. Neuropeak Pro (website), accessed January 15, 2022, neuropeakpro .com.

8. Nancy Lopez, personal communication, February 2021.

9. NHL Trade Rumors (website), "Blackhawks' Duncan Keith

Opened Up About His Secrets," February 15, 2021, nhltraderumors.
me/2021/02/blackhawks-duncan-keith-opened-up-about.html.

10. Jim Nelford, personal communication.

CHAPTER FOUR: CHANGING PROGRAMS – THE RELEASE REFLEX

1. SJ, personal communication.
2. Brainy Quote (website), accessed January 15, 2021, brainyquote.
   com/authors/lee-westwood-quotes.
3. Nancy Lopez, personal communication, February 2021.
4. Dustin Johnson, me and my golf interview, March 2, 2020.
5. Jaime Diaz, "What Made Tiger Woods Great?" *Golf Digest*,
   January 23, 2018, www.golfdigest.com/story/what-made-tiger-
   woods-great-and-can-again-jaime-diaz-magazine.
6. Tim Gallwey, "The Inner Game of Golf; Putt Like a
   Pro," November 2, 2015, YouTube video, youtube.com/
   watch?v=Jz4X2xQmgIg.
7. W. Timothy Gallwey, *The Inner Game of Tennis*, (New York:
   Random House, 1974) and W. Timothy Gallwey, *The Inner Game of
   Golf*, (New York: Random House, 1981).
8. Pinterest (website), accessed January 16, 2022, pinterest.com/
   pin/844002786397241605.
9. Jeff, personal communication.
10. Alexander, personal communication.
11. Brainy Quote (website), accessed January 15, 2022, brainyquote.
    com/quotes/bobby-jones.
12. Brian Danny, personal communication, December 2020.
13. Pinterest (website), accessed January 15, pinterest.ch/
    pin/817544138586159389.
14. Johnette Howard, "How Sports Science Explains Greg Norman's
    1996 Masters Meltdown," ESPN (website), March 29, 2016, espn.
    com/golf/story/_/id/15091501/how-sports-science-explains-greg-
    norman-1996-masters-meltdown.

SECTION THREE: RIGHT FOCUS

1. Ten Golf, "Lydia Ko: Winner Press Conference 2021 Lotte Championship LPGA Tour," April 18, 2021, YouTube video, youtube.com/watch?v=Iu-KRFLu38E.

CHAPTER FIVE: POWER THINKING

1. Dick Zokol, personal communication, February 2021.
2. Quotefancy (website), accessed January 15, 2022, quotefancy.com/quote160963/david-leadbetter/your-final -goal.
3. Quotefancy (website), accessed January 15, 2022, quotefancy.com/quote/1619136/curtis-strange.
4. Jayne Storey, "Breathing to Win — Chi-Power Golf," *Golf Monthly* (website), October 16, 2008, golfmonthly.com/tips/fitness/breathing-to-win-chi-power-golf-21804.
5. Jaime Diaz, "What Made Tiger Woods Great?," *Golf Digest*, January 23, 2018, www.golfdigest.com/story/what-made-tiger-woods-great-and-can-again-jaime-diaz-magazine.
6. Ibid.

CHAPTER SIX: HIGH-PERFORMANCE IMAGERY

1. Brainy Quote (website), accessed January 15, 2022, brainyquote.com/authors/albert-einstein-quotes.
2. Eric Wang, personal communication.
3. Harvey Penick, *Harvey Penick's Little Red Book: Lessons and Teachings from a Lifetime in Golf,* (New York: Simon & Schuster, 2012).
4. TaylorMade Golf, "Tiger Woods' Nine Windows," September 21, 2021, YouTube video, youtube.com/watch?v=qomj9AdzoJw.
5. Golf Post Editors, "Dustin Johnson: 'As a Kid I Always Dreamed about Being a Masters-Champion,'" *Golf Post*, November 16, 2020,

golfpost.com/cms/dustin-johnson-as-a-kid-i-always-dreamed-about-being-a-masters-champion.

6. Nancy Lopez, personal communication, February 2021.

7. Mississippi Sports Hall of Fame and Museum (website), "Remembering Colonel George Robert Hall," June 3, 2014, msfame.com/remembering-colonel-george-robert-hall.

8. The Golf Experience (website), "Jack Nicklaus Quotes," accessed January 15, 2021, the-golf-experience.com/jack-nicklaus-quotes .html.

9. Jim Flick and Jack Nicklaus, "Jim Flick And Jack Nicklaus: Go to The Movies," *Golf Digest*, April 27, 2010, golfdigest.com/story/flick -nicklaus-film.

10. Redhawk Golf Course (website), accessed January 15, 2021, redhawkgolfcourse.com/instruction/.

11. Eric Wang, personal communication.

12. Harvey Penick, *Harvey Penick's Little Red Book: Lessons and Teachings from a Lifetime in Golf*, (New York: Simon & Schuster, 2012).

13. Geoff Shackelford, "Ben Crenshaw Shares His Tips to Improving Your Putting Game," *Golfweek*, May 8, 2019, golfweek.usatoday. com/2019/05/08/ben-crenshaw-golf-putting-tips.

14. Cameron Morfit, "Garcia Putting with His Eyes Closed," PGA Tour (website), October 2, 2020, pgatour.com/news/2020/10/02/ sergio-garcia-putting-eyes-closed-round-2-sanderson-farms-championship-country-club-of-jackson.html.

15. Pinterest (website), accessed January 15, pinterest.com/ pin/975311481607231 96.

CHAPTER SEVEN: EXCEPTIONAL PERFORMANCES – THE SUB-60 CLUB

1. Rhein Gibson, personal communication.

2. W. Timothy Gallwey, *The Inner Game of Golf*, (New York: Random House, 1981).

3. Alexander Hughes, personal communication.

4. Alex Myers, "Remembering Al Geiberger's 59 on Its 35th Anniversary," *Golf Digest*, June 10, 2012, golfdigest.com/story/remembering-al-geibergers-59-on-its-35th-anniversary.

5. LPGA, "15 Years Later, Annika Sorenstam Remembers 59," March 16, 2016, YouTube video, youtube.com/watch?v=YNGvp8JiJXE.

6. PGA Tour, "Highlights from Jim Furyk's 58," August 7, 2016, facebook.com/watch/?v=10153543289176330.

7. John Feinstein, "David Duval Reflects on His 59: 'The Easiest Round of Golf I Ever Played,'" *Golf Digest*, January 23, 2021, golfdigest.com/story/david-duval-50-bob-hope-pga-tour-history.

8. PGA Tour, "Scottie Scheffler Discusses 59 in Round 2 of The Northern Trust," August 21, 2020, pgatour.com/video/2020/08/21/scottie-schefflers-interview-after-round-1-of-the-northern-trust.html.

9. Robert Thompson, "Abbotsford's Adam Hadwin Shoots 59," Global News (website), January 21, 2017, globalnews.ca/news/3197335/abbotsfords-adam-hadwin-shoots-13-under-59-in-careerbuilder-challenge.

10. Ron Futrell, "Ron Futrell Reports on Chip Beck Shoots a 59," October 11, 1991, YouTube video, youtube.com/watch?v=wWVtX_PqVjo.

11. Ten Golf, "Adam Hadwin Thursday Flash Interview 2020 The Masters Tournament — Round 1," November 12, 2020, YouTube video, youtube.com/watch?v=eo7Bz7wFrno.

CHAPTER EIGHT: COMMITMENT

1. Jaime Diaz, "What Made Tiger Woods Great?" *Golf Digest*, January 23, 2018, www.golfdigest.com/story/what-made-tiger-woods-great-and-can-again-jaime-diaz-magazine.

2. Pinterest (website), accessed January 15, 2022, pinterest.ca/pin/268104984037398016.

3. Quotefancy (website), accessed January 15, 2022, quotefancy.com/ quote/1763405/Matt-Kuchar-Even-if-you-finish-the-year-at-No-1-in-the-world-and-Tiger-Woods-has-done.

4. Howard E. Ferguson and Gary Schwab, *The Edge: The Guide to Fulfilling Dreams, Maximizing Success and Enjoying a Lifetime of Achievement*, (Cleveland, OH: Getting the Edge Co., 1990).

5. Quotefancy (website), accessed January 15, 2022, quotefancy.com/ quote/1344289/jack-nicklaus.

6. Ben Everill, "Matsuyama Shares Lead after First Round at Players," Reuters, May 7, 2015, reuters.com/article/us-golf-pga-idUSKBN0NS28S20150508.

7. Brainy Quote (website), accessed January 15, 2022, brainyquote. com/quotes/calvin-coolidge/414555.

8. Love Expands (website), accessed January 16, 2022, loveexpands. com/author/bobby-knight/.

9. Nancy Lopez, personal communication, February 2021.

10. Heidi Grant Halvorson, "How did Tiger Woods Ignore that Plane?: Strategies for Fighting off Distraction," *Psychology Today* (online), April 9, 2010, psychologytoday.com/ca/blog/the-science-success/201004/how-did-tiger-woods-ignore-plane.

11. Ibid.

CHAPTER NINE: CONFIDENCE

1. Rhein Gibson, personal communication, January 2021.

2. Golf Channel, "Positive Nerves Push Collin Morikawa to Open Championship Victory, July 18, 2021, YouTube video, youtube.com/ watch?v=vumRG6ILWBA.

3. Golf Channel, "Collin Morikawa Owes 'Everything' to the Scottish Open for 149 Open Win," July 19, 2021, youtube.com/ watch?v=NtYz5XJey-0.

4. Ibid.

5. Ten Golf , "Lydia Ko: Winner Press Conference 2021 Lotte

Championship LPGA Tour," April 18, 2021, YouTube video, youtube.com/watch?v=Iu-KRFLu38E.

6. SCOREGolf, "How Corey Found His Aggression," May 14, 2019, YouTube video, youtube.com/watch?v=67xIokugVOo.

7. Markus Naslund, personal communication.

8. Jake Humphrey and Damian Hughes, hosts, "Paul McGinley: Empower Not Overpower," *The High Performance Podcast*, video podcast, August 9, 2021, youtube.com/watch?v=Gy85UTzRTG4.

9. CoachUp Nation (website), accessed January 16, 2022, coachup.com/nation/articles/the-separation-is-in-the-preparation-5-steps-to-be-successful-like-seattle-seahawks-quarterback-russell-wilson.

10. Quotefancy (website), accessed January 16, 2022, quotefancy.com/quote/1357904/Bill-Parcells-The-more-you-prepare-beforehand-the-more-relaxed-and-creative-and-effective.

11. Brainy Quote (website), accessed January 15, 2022, brainyquote.com/authors/roger-staubach-quote.

12. Golf Channel, "Collin Morikawa Owes 'Everything' to the Scottish Open for 149 Open Win," July 19, 2021, YouTube video, youtube.com/watch?v=NtYz5XJey-0.

13. Jim Nelford, personal communication.

14. Luke Kerr-Dineen, "This Is Jordan Spieth's New Magic Move — And Why Slicers Should Try It," Golf, April 5, 2021, apple.news/ASXzSqVZ6TUeWgzwKIpOzgw.

15. Sam Weinman, "What Are The Yips?: Experts Say It's Not Just In Your Head," *Golf Digest* (website), April 8, 2016, golfdigest.com/story/what-are-the-yips-experts-say-its-not-just-in-your-head.

CHAPTER TEN: IDENTITY

1. Cameron Morfit, "Tony Finau Back In Win Column at The Northern Trust," PGA Tour (website), August 23, 2021, pgatour

.com/news/2021/08/23/tony-finau-win-playoff-cameron-smith-the
-northern-trust-liberty-national.html.

2. Gervais Rioux, personal communication.

3. Golf Channel, "Collin Morikawa Owes 'Everything' to the
Scottish Open for 149 Open Win," July 19, 2021, YouTube video,
youtube.com/watch?v=NtYz5XJey-0.

4. Golf Channel (website), "Watch: Dustin Johnson Gets Emotional
After Masters Victory," November 15, 2020, golfchannel.com/
news/watch-dustin-johnson-gets-emotional-after-masters-
victory.

5. Brainy Quote (website), accessed January 15, 2022, brainyquote.
Com/quotes/sam-snead-380687.

6. Adam Schupak, "Phil Mickelson: 'If I Don't Play Well Early On,
I'll Start To Re-evaluate' Future On PGA Tour," *Golfweek*, January
20, 2021, golfweek.usatoday.com/2021/01/20/phil-mickelson-if-i-
dont-play-well-early-on-ill-re-evaluate-future.

7. Bill Walker, personal communication.

CHAPTER ELEVEN: BALANCE AND LIFESTYLE

1. Nancy Lopez, personal communication, February 2021.

2. Adam Stanley, "Henderson Hoping This Is Her Year at the U.S.
Women's Open," USGA (website), December 2, 2020, usga.org/
content/usga/home-page/championships/2020/u-s--women-s-open/
articles/henderson-hoping-this-is-her-year-at-the-u-s--women-s-
open-.html.

3. Jane McClenaghan, "Nutrition: Good Nutrition For Golfers —
Eat Your Way To A Better Game," *The Irish News* (website),
July 20, 2019, irishnews.com/lifestyle/2019/07/20/news/
nutrition-good-nutrition-for-golfers---eat-your-way-to-a-
better-game-1664363.

4. Ibid.

5. Ibid.

6. Ibid.

7. Dylan Dethier, "Bryson DeChambeau's Everyday Diet (7 Protein Shakes!) Will Shock You," *Golf* (website), June 30, 2020, golf.com/lifestyle/bryson-dechambeaus-diet-protein-shakes-calories.

8. Famous Quotes (website), accessed January 15, 2022, famousquotes.com/quotes-about-concentrating.

9. B. Coleman, personal communication.

10. Guy Yocom, "My Shot: Moe Norman," *Golf Digest* (website), July 7, 2007, golfdigest.com/story/myshot_gd0411.

11. Jon Kabat-Zinn, "Everyday Mindfulness with Jon Kabat-Zinn," Mindful (website), accessed January 16, 2022, mindful.org/everyday-mindfulness-with-jon-kabat-zinn.

12. Brainy Quote (website), accessed January 16, 2022, brainyquote.com/quotes/bubba_watson_430276.

13. Ten Golf , "Lydia Ko: Winner Press Conference 2021 Lotte Championship LPGA Tour," April 18, 2021, YouTube video, youtube.com/watch?v=Iu-KRFLu38E.

14. LPGA (website), "Nelly Korda Final Interview at the 2021 Gainbridge LPGA," February 28, 2021, lpga.com/videos/2021/nelly-korda-final-interview-at-the-2021-gainbridge-lpga.

15. Matt Craddock, "Get To Know Nelly Korda's Caddie, Jason McDede, Here," *Golf Monthly* (website), April 17, 2021, golfmonthly.com/features/the-game/who-is-nelly-kordas-caddie-229274.

16. PGA Tour, "Max Homa Talks Recent Mental Changes to Improve Life and Golf," Facebook, January 23, 2021, facebook.com/page/10643196329/search/?q=Perspective.

17. Golf Channel, "Positive Nerves Push Collin Morikawa to Open Championship Victory," July 18, 2021, YouTube video, youtube.com/watch?v=vumRG6ILWBA.

CHAPTER TWELVE: INDIVIDUAL DIFFERENCES

1. Warrior Mind Coach (website), accessed January 23, 2022, warriormindcoach.com/?s=pressure+creates.
2. Tom Pilcher, "How Dustin Johnson's Speedy Approach Could Help Golf's Pace of Play," CNN website, January 5, 2021, cnn.com/2021/01/05/golf/speed-golf-dustin-johnson-bryson-dechambeau-spc-spt-intl/index.html.
3. Brainy Quote, accessed January 23, 2022, brainyquote.com/authors/nancy-lopez-quotes.
4. Bubba, personal communication.
5. Sean, personal communication.

CHAPTER THIRTEEN: TRANSFERRING MENTAL SKILLS

1. Cliff Ronning, personal communication.
2. Morris Lukowich, personal communication.
3. Quotefancy (website), accessed January 16, 20222, quotefancy.com/quote/1356734/Arnold-Palmer-The-whole-secret-to-mastering-the-game-of-golf-and-this-applies-to-the.
4. Bret Hedican, personal communication.
5. Leroy Irvin, personal communication.
6. Mark Jerue, personal communication.

Dr. Saul L. Miller is one of North America's leading sport and performance psychologists and the author of nine books on performance and well-being. Dr. Miller consults with individuals, sport teams, corporations, and health organizations across North America and Europe. The focus of his work is on enhancing performance, team building, and helping people achieve success while dealing with pressure, stress, and change effectively.

In addition to working with the PGA Tour, NCAA, and recreational golfers, Saul has consulted with the New York Mets, Seattle Mariners, Los Angeles Dodgers, Rams, Clippers, and Kings, St. Louis Blues, Vancouver Canucks, Nashville Predators, dozens of European professional teams, and Olympians from the USA, Canada, and Europe in over thirty different sports.

In business, his clients come from management, manufacturing, sales, and service. He has consulted with financial services, technology, insurance, and the building, automotive, and service industries, as well as health care.

There is no one in North America with more "hands-on" experience facilitating success and well-being. Dr. Miller's clients have set records, won championships and gold medals, increased sales volumes by 100%, improved management "coaching" effectiveness, and improved their health and well-being.

A graduate of McGill University and the Institute of Psychiatry at the University of London (Ph.D. Clinical Psychology), his work reflects his study of Eastern disciplines, Western psychological thinking, and over forty years of front-line experience consulting with some of the world's top performers.